Discover Barbados : Your Ultimate Travel Guide 2024

Discover Paradise in the Caribbean with the Most Comprehensive Guide for 2024"

Eric Jacobs

1

Table Of Content

Chapter 1

Planning Your Trip
A Comprehensive Guide to Planning an Unforgettable Trip to Barbados.
Essential Packing Guide for Your Visit to Barbados and Suggested Items to Buy.

Chapter 2

Visa and Entry Requirements
Visa and Entry Requirements in Barbados: Custom Recommendations and Visa Application.
Dos and Don'ts of Barbados You'll Never Forget

Chapter 3

Safety Requirements Providing a Safe and Enjoyable Visit: Barbados Safety Requirements

Chapter 9

Accommodation Options Accommodation Options in Barbados: Budgeting for Rental Homestay and Hotels.

Chapter 10

Best Time to Visit Barbados for Perfect Weather And Memorable Experiences.

Chapter 11

Barbados, Top Tourist Destinations You Must See.

Chapter 12

Dining and entertainment restaurants in Barbados

Chapter 13

Hidden Gems in Barbados: A Treasure Hunt Through Its Unknown Gems

Introduction

QBarbados, the diamond of the Caribbean, entices explorers with its immaculate sea shores, dynamic culture, and a rich history that traverses hundreds of years. This island heaven, frequently alluded to as "Little Britain" because of its pioneer history, is an embroidery of normal excellence and warm neighborliness. In "Discover Barbados: Your Ultimate Travel Guide 2024," we welcome you to set out on an extraordinary excursion through this captivating objective, where each corner is a disclosure and each second is a chance for experience.

A Caribbean Heaven Calls

The appeal of Barbados is obvious, drawing guests from around the world to its sun-kissed shores. As the easternmost Caribbean island, Barbados partakes in an ideal place in the core of the Lesser Antilles, making it a tropical safe house with unspoiled weather conditions lasting through the year. This lavish, paradisiacal island is a mosaic of scenes, from the quiet, palm-bordered sea shores of the west coast to the rough precipices and strong Atlantic floods of the east coast.

A Social Mixture

Barbados isn't simply a banquet for the faculties through its regular excellence yet in addition through its dynamic culture. With a rich history profoundly impacted by African, English, and West Indian legacy, the island's way of life is a bright embroidery of customs, music, and cooking. From the cadenced beats of Calypso and Soca music to the tempting kinds of Bajan cooking, guests will find a remarkable combination of customs that spellbinds and charms.

History and Legacy

This movement guide will take you on an excursion through Barbados' interesting history, from its days as an English settlement to its development as a free country. Investigate noteworthy destinations, for example, Bridgetown, an UNESCO World Legacy Site, where exceptionally old structures stand as observers to the island's past. Reveal the tale of the sugar business, which assumed a vital part in forming the country's character.

Extraordinary Encounters Anticipate

For those looking for experience, Barbados offers a variety of thrilling encounters. Jump into the perfectly clear waters to investigate dynamic coral reefs and submerged wrecks, sail along the shore, or ride the waves at widely acclaimed surf spots. Find the island's rich inside, where climbing and investigation lead to stowed away fortunes like Harrison's Cavern and Welchman Lobby Gorge.

Your Ultimate Travel Guide

"Discover Barbados: Your Ultimate Travel Guide 2024" has been carefully created to guarantee your process is consistent and loaded up with advancing encounters. From reasonable data on facilities, eating, and transportation to insider tips on must-visit attractions and unexpected, yet invaluable treasures, this guide is your confided in buddy. Whether you're an independent explorer, a couple looking for a heartfelt escape, a family looking for experience, or a set of experiences lover, Barbados offers something for everybody.

Go along with us as we explore through this dazzling island, furnishing you with important experiences and nearby information. Allow the experience to start, as we take you on a visit through the most pleasant sea shores, the most rich eating recognizes, the most exciting exercises, and the most improving social encounters Barbados brings to the table. Prepare to leave on the vacation that could only be described as epic as you Discover Barbados - Your Ultimate Travel Guide 2024.

Barbados overview

Barbados, situated in the eastern Caribbean, is a little island country with a rich history, shocking regular magnificence, and a lively culture. Known for its unspoiled sea shores, warm environment, and inviting individuals, Barbados is a famous traveler objective. We should dive into a definite outline of this charming island country.

Geology:
Barbados is the most easterly island in the Caribbean and is arranged in the Atlantic Sea, not the Caribbean Ocean. It covers an area of around 166 square miles (430 square kilometers). The island is generally level, with delicately moving slopes and a shocking shoreline that is bordered with white-sand sea shores and coral reefs.

Capital and Urban communities:
The capital city of Barbados is Bridgetown, situated on the southwestern coast. Bridgetown is the social and monetary center of the island, including noteworthy provincial design, lively business sectors, and a clamoring harbor. Other significant towns on the island incorporate Holetown, Oistins,

and Speightstown, each offering novel encounters and attractions.

History:
Barbados has an entrancing history, having been occupied by native Amerindian people groups prior to being colonized by the English in the seventeenth 100 years. The island's set of experiences is interlaced with the sugar business, as it was a significant maker of sugar stick during the pilgrim period, prompting the importation of African slaves. Barbados acquired its freedom from England in 1966 and is presently a parliamentary majority rules system with an established government, where the English ruler fills in as the formal head of state.

Culture:
Barbadian culture is a rich mix of African, English, and West Indian impacts. The island's music, dance, and celebrations, for example, Yield Over, mirror this social combination. Barbados is additionally known for its culinary joys, with dishes like flying fish and cou being nearby top picks. Individuals of Barbados, known as Bajans, are known for their warm neighborliness and amicability.

The travel industry:
The travel industry is a crucial industry in Barbados, drawing in guests from around the world. The island offers a different scope of attractions, from perfect sea shores like Crane Ocean side and Base Inlet to notable locales like St. Nicholas Convent and George Washington House. Water sports, including swimming, scuba plunging, and cruising, are additionally famous exercises.

Economy:
The Barbadian economy is enhanced, with areas like the travel industry, monetary administrations, and agribusiness assuming pivotal parts. The island is known for its seaward banking and global business administrations, which contribute altogether to its economy. Horticulture, once based on sugar, has moved to different harvests like sugarcane, bananas, and yams.

Schooling:
Barbados puts major areas of strength for on instruction and has a high proficiency rate. It flaunts an advanced schooling system, with both public and confidential foundations, including the College of the West Indies, Cavern Slope Grounds.

Regular Magnificence:
The island's regular magnificence is quite possibly of its most striking element. Barbados is known for its lavish professional flowerbeds, for example, Andromeda Nurseries, and underground ponders like Harrison's Cavern. It is likewise home to different natural life and marine life, making it an extraordinary objective for eco-the travel industry.

Transportation:
Barbados has an advanced transportation framework. Grantley Adams Global Air terminal is the essential entryway to the island, serving various worldwide flights. The street network is broad, and transports and cabs are promptly accessible for getting around.

Barbados offers an enrapturing mix of regular magnificence, rich history, and lively culture. Whether you're looking for a loosening up oceanside escape, an investigation of history and culture, or an experience in nature, Barbados brings something to the table for each voyager. This beguiling island country keeps on charming guests with its warm cordiality and amazing scenes.

<u>Brief History Of Barbados</u>

Barbados, a pleasant island country situated in the Caribbean, has a rich and dynamic history that traverses hundreds of years. Its story starts some time before European colonization, as the island was initially possessed by the Arawak and Carib people groups. In the late fifteenth 100 years, Spanish wayfarers were among the primary Europeans to go to Barbados, yet it was only after the seventeenth century that the English laid out their presence, making a permanent imprint on the island's set of experiences.

Pre-Provincial Barbados: Before European contact, Barbados was home to the Arawak and Carib native clans. These local individuals flourished with the island, living off its lavish vegetation and fishing in its encompassing waters.

European Investigation: Spanish guides, including Pedro Campos and Pedro Colón, visited Barbados in the late fifteenth 100 years. Nonetheless, the island's absence of valuable metals beat Spanish colonization endeavors down.

English Colonization: The main English endeavor showed up in Barbados in 1625, drove by Commander John Powell. The English Crown asserted the island, and its settlement started decisively. The early economy depended on tobacco and cotton development, yet sugar turned into the predominant yield by the mid-seventeenth hundred years. This change prompted an expanded interest for oppressed work.

Transoceanic Slave Exchange: Barbados assumed a urgent part in the overseas slave exchange, with endless Africans effectively brought to the island to chip away at sugar manors. This dull period in history lastingly affected the island's segment and social piece.

Financial Flourishing: By the eighteenth hundred years, Barbados had become one of the most affluent English states because of its rewarding sugar industry. The island's ranches were profoundly beneficial, and sugar sends out were popular in Europe.

Liberation and Abrogation: Servitude was canceled in Barbados in 1834, trailed by full liberation in 1838. This undeniable a huge defining moment in the island's set of experiences, as previous oppressed individuals looked for open doors in different callings and added to the island's turn of events.

Freedom: Barbados kept on developing all through the twentieth hundred years. In 1966, it accomplished freedom from England, turning into a sovereign country and taking on a parliamentary majority rule government.

Current Barbados: Since freedom, Barbados has gained exceptional headway in different fields, including training, medical care, and the travel industry. The island has drawn in guests from around the world who come to partake in its shocking sea shores, lively culture, and warm accommodation.

Ongoing Turns of events: In 2021, Barbados stood out as truly newsworthy when it reported its change from an established government to a republic. This critical sacred change denoted another time in the island's set of experiences.

Culture and Customs: Barbados has a rich social legacy impacted by its African, English, and West Indian roots. The island's way of life is commended through music, dance, and celebrations. The vivacious rhythms of calypso and reggae can frequently be heard at neighborhood social occasions, including the incredibly popular Yield Over Celebration, a lively festival commending the finish of the sugarcane gather season.

Schooling and Proficiency: Barbados puts areas of strength for on instruction, with a high education rate and an advanced schooling system. The island is home to the College of the West Indies, which has grounds across the Caribbean, including Barbados.

Medical services: Barbados flaunts a vigorous medical services framework with current offices and an emphasis on general wellbeing. It has taken critical steps in giving quality medical care administrations to its residents and guests.

The travel industry: The travel industry assumes an essential part in the island's economy. Barbados draws in guests from around the world with its staggering sea shores, coral reefs, and verifiable attractions. The island offers a large number of facilities, from extravagance resorts to store inns.

Culinary Joys: Barbadian cooking, frequently alluded to as "Bajan" food, includes a blend of flavors impacted by the island's set of experiences. Well known dishes incorporate flying fish and cou, pepperpot, and fish cakes. Nearby rum is likewise a number one, and guests can visit rum refineries to find out about the island's refining history.

Ecological Drives: Barbados has been proactive in tending to ecological worries, including environmental change and safeguarding its regular excellence. Endeavors to safeguard the coral reefs, oversee marine preservation regions, and advance feasible the travel industry are continuous.

Republic Status: In 2021, Barbados impacted the world forever by progressing from a protected government to a republic. This established change included the evacuation of the English ruler as the head of state and the arrangement of a Barbadian president. The move denoted a critical stage towards full power and self-administration.

Worldwide Discretion: As an autonomous country, Barbados keeps up with conciliatory relations with nations all over the planet and is a functioning individual from different global associations, including the Unified Countries and the Province of Countries.

Monetary Enhancement: While sugar was generally the foundation of Barbados' economy, the island has broadened its financial exercises. Notwithstanding the travel industry, areas like money, data innovation, and environmentally friendly power have become progressively significant as of late.

Today, Barbados is a flourishing and socially different country known for its pleasant scenes, dynamic celebrations, and a profound appreciation for its verifiable heritage. Its set of experiences is a demonstration of the strength of its kin and their capacity to beat difficulties while protecting their special social legacy.

killer Apps in Bardados

Barbados, the pleasant island heaven in the Caribbean, is known for its shocking sea shores, energetic culture, and warm neighborliness. To take full advantage of your Barbados experience, you'll need to have some fundamental applications readily available. Whether you're a traveler or a nearby, these applications can assist you with exploring the island, find unlikely treasures, and partake in your opportunity without limit. In this article, we'll investigate the best executioner applications that are an unquestionable requirement for anybody in Barbados.

Google Guides:
Route is significant while investigating Barbados, and Google Guides is a basic instrument for this reason. It gives continuous headings, traffic updates, and data on nearby organizations, making it simple to track down your direction to wonderful sea shores, notable locales, and extraordinary eating spots.

Barbados Pocket Guide:

This application is your computerized local escort to Barbados. It offers a far reaching rundown of attractions, cafés, occasions, and facilities. You can get to definite depictions, photographs, and surveys, guaranteeing you don't miss any of the island's must-visit places.

Bajan Sun On the web:
Barbados is well known for its sun-splashed sea shores, and Bajan Sun Online gives ongoing data about the island's weather patterns, including temperature, UV record, and weather conditions figures. It's a convenient application for arranging your outside exercises.

BeachSafe Barbados:
Prior to making a beeline for an ocean side, you can really take a look at its security status with BeachSafe Barbados. The application gives exceptional data on water conditions, including wave level, undertows, and any warnings or alerts.

Bajans in a hurry:
This application is a mother lode of data about nearby occasions, bargains, and social encounters. It's ideal for tracking down the most recent

happenings on the island, from live events to craftsmanship presentations.

Moovit:
Getting around Barbados by open transportation? Moovit is your go-to application for transport timetables and courses. It guarantees you can without much of a stretch investigate the island while setting aside time and cash.

WhatsApp:
Remain associated with loved ones with WhatsApp, the well known informing application. It's regularly utilized for correspondence in Barbados, making it a fundamental apparatus for the two sightseers and occupants.

Bajan Chimes:
For foodies and culinary devotees, Bajan Chimes is a phenomenal application. It offers data on neighborhood diners, including menus and client audits. You can find the best places to appreciate Barbadian cooking.

WhatsApp Food Conveyance:

At the point when you're in the state of mind for a scrumptious feast yet don't have any desire to eat out, WhatsApp Food Conveyance interfaces you to neighborhood cafés that offer conveyance administrations, guaranteeing you can appreciate Barbadian flavors from the solace of your facilities.

Barbados is a charming objective with a great deal to offer, and having the right applications can improve your experience on the island. Whether you're searching for route help, neighborhood experiences, or culinary pleasures, these executioner applications will assist you with capitalizing on your time in Barbados. Thus, before you set out to this tropical heaven, try to download and introduce these applications to guarantee a smooth and extraordinary visit.

Chapter 1

Planning Your Trip
A Comprehensive Guide to Planning an
Unforgettable Trip to Barbados.

Barbados, frequently alluded to as the "Jewel of the Caribbean," is a heaven island situated in the eastern Caribbean Ocean. Its pleasant sea shores, dynamic culture, and warm cordiality make it an ideal objective for explorers looking for a significant escape. This exhaustive aide will assist you with arranging your excursion to Barbados, covering everything from what's in store, what should be done, transportation, identification prerequisites, and that's only the tip of the iceberg.

Barbados Initially

Barbados is a little island country in the Caribbean, known for its white-sand sea shores, completely clear waters, and a rich social legacy. The island's true language is English, and it has a heat and humidity, making it an all year objective. Barbados is a famous decision for both unwinding and experience, offering a mix of regular magnificence and energetic metropolitan life.

Identification and Visa

To enter Barbados, you'll require a legitimate identification. Guarantee that your identification is in great shape and has no less than a half year of legitimacy remaining. Contingent upon your identity, you might require a visa. Check with the Barbados Migration Division or the Barbados Consulate in your country to decide your visa prerequisites.

Sans visa Passage

Numerous voyagers from North America, Europe, and the Republic nations can enter Barbados without a visa for short stays, regularly as long as 90 days. Be that as it may, the permitted span can change, so really take a look at the particular necessities for your country.

Customs and Migration

Upon appearance, you'll go through customs and migration. Finish up the essential appearance frames and be ready to pronounce any things of significant worth you're conveying. Barbados is for the most part inviting to sightseers, yet adhering to the traditions and movement guidelines is fundamental.

Best Chance to Visit

Barbados partakes in a warm, heat and humidity all year, with temperatures averaging around 86°F (30°C).

The high season for the travel industry is from mid-December to mid-April, offering the most charming climate. In any case, it's likewise the most costly opportunity to visit. The off-top season, from June to November, is more spending plan agreeable yet can be rainier because of the typhoon season.

Celebrations and Occasions

Think about visiting Barbados during its celebrations, like Harvest Over in July and August, a vivacious festival of music, dance, and culture. Barbados additionally has different regattas, food celebrations, and widespread developments consistently.

Barbados offers an extensive variety of convenience choices to suit various spending plans. From extravagance resorts on the west coast to comfortable guesthouses and excursion rentals, you can track down the ideal spot to remain. Well known regions for convenience incorporate St. Lawrence Hole, Bridgetown, and the west coast, which is known for its upscale retreats.

Reservations

It's fitting to book your convenience ahead of time, particularly during the high season, to get the best rates and accessibility. Utilize legitimate internet booking stages or work with a travel planner to track down the best housing for your excursion.

Getting to Barbados

Most worldwide explorers show up in Barbados through Grantley Adams Global Air terminal (BGI). The air terminal is very much associated with significant urban areas in North America, Europe, and the Caribbean. Aircrafts like American Carriers, English Aviation routes, and Caribbean Aircrafts offer standard trips to the island.

Getting Around the Island

Rental Vehicles: Leasing a vehicle is a helpful choice to investigate Barbados at your own speed. Drive on the left half of the street, and be mindful on limited and winding streets.

Public Transportation: Barbados offers an effective and reasonable public transport framework. You can likewise utilize shared vans known as "ZR vans" for brief excursions.

Taxis: Cabs are promptly accessible and can be recruited for little excursions or entire day visits. Continuously affirm the charge with the driver prior to leaving.

Bikes and Bikes: A few sightseers select leasing bikes or bikes for a more daring method for investigating the island.

Ocean side Happiness

Barbados is popular for its staggering sea shores. Try not to miss:

Crane Ocean side: Known for its stunning precipices and unblemished sands.
Carlisle Sound: Ideal for water sports and swimming.
Mullins Ocean side: Incredible for unwinding and water exercises.
Authentic Locales

Investigate the island's rich history at places like:

Harrison's Cavern: A characteristic marvel with underground caverns and streams.
St. Nicholas Monastery: A noteworthy estate house and rum refinery.
Barbados Gallery and Authentic Culture: Offers bits of knowledge into the island's legacy.
Experience and Watersports

Surfing: Barbados has top notch surf spots like Soup Bowl.
Swimming and Jumping: Find lively marine life free waters.
Sailboat Travels: Sail along the coast and swim with ocean turtles.
Social Encounters

Oistins Fish Fry: Enjoy neighborhood cooking and experience Barbadian nightlife.
Mount Gay Rum Refinery Visit: Find out about the island's rum-production legacy.
Crop Over Celebration: Join the excellent festival of music and dance.
Nature and Untamed life

Bloom Woods Greenhouses: Investigate lavish gardens and strolling trails.
Untamed life Save: Experience green monkeys in a characteristic natural surroundings.

Cash

The authority cash in Barbados is the Barbadian Dollar (BBD). Most organizations likewise acknowledge the U.S. Dollar, and Mastercards are generally utilized. ATMs are accessible all through the island for helpful money withdrawals.

Planning

Barbados can be a costly objective, however arranging an outing that suits your budget is conceivable. Be ready at greater expenses at eateries and resorts on the west coast contrasted with additional reasonable choices on the south and east drifts.

Wellbeing Safeguards

Guarantee you're fully informed regarding routine immunizations and consider extra inoculations in light of your itinerary items. The island's faucet water is protected to drink, yet you can likewise buy filtered water.

Mosquito Assurance

Avoid potential risk against mosquitoes, which are generally dynamic at day break and nightfall. Use bug repellent and consider remaining in facilities with screened windows and cooling.

Security

Barbados is by and large a protected objective for voyagers, however practicing standard precautions is fundamental. Try not to show important things, be wary around evening time, and secure your assets.

Regard Local people

Barbadians are known for their neighborliness and amenability. Recognize their way of life and customs, and welcome individuals with a warm "Hello" or "Good evening."

Clothing standard

Pack clothing appropriate for the warm environment. While beachwear is OK at the ocean side, conceal while visiting towns and cafés.

Driving Manners

In the event that you intend to lease a vehicle, drive on the road and give way to one side at traffic circles.

Barbados offers a magnificent mix of regular magnificence, social encounters, and warm friendliness. Whether you're looking for unwinding on the oceanfront.

Essential Packing Guide for Your Visit to Barbados and Suggested Items to Buy.

Absolutely! Here is an itemized content on the fundamental pressing aide for your visit to Barbados and recommended things to purchase:

Fundamental Pressing Aide for Your Visit to Barbados
Presentation
Barbados, with its dazzling sea shores, lively culture, and warm climate, is a fantasy objective for some. Whether you're arranging a loosening up ocean side get-away or an undertaking filled trip, pressing right is essential to guarantee you have an important and tranquil experience. This fundamental pressing aide for your visit to Barbados will assist you with getting ready for your excursion and guarantee you're good to go for the island's interesting environment.

Apparel and Footwear
Swimwear: You'll invest a ton of energy near the ocean, so pack different bathing suits. Women could likewise need to incorporate a concealment for beachside feasting.

Light Apparel: Pack lightweight, breathable attire like shorts, sundresses, and shirts. Barbados is hot and damp, so focus on solace.

Footwear: Agreeable shoes or flip-flops are an unquestionable requirement for the ocean side, yet you'll likewise require shut toe shoes for investigating. Shoes or strolling shoes are great for climbing and touring.

Downpour Stuff: Barbados encounters irregular downpour showers. A minimal, convenient downpour coat or umbrella is smart.

Evening Clothing: Assuming you intend to partake in Barbados' nightlife, pack a few shrewd relaxed outfits. A few eateries and clubs have clothing standards.

Sun Insurance
Sunscreen: The sun in Barbados can be serious. Pack high-SPF sunscreen to shield your skin from sun related burn.

Sun Cap and Shades: A wide-overflowed cap and UV-defensive shades are fundamental for added sun security.

Ocean side Towel: While numerous lodgings give ocean side towels, having your own can be advantageous.

Travel Records
Identification and Visa: Guarantee your identification is substantial for no less than a half year past your arranged flight date. Actually take a look at the visa prerequisites for your country.

Travel Protection: Think about buying travel protection that covers health related crises, trip abrogations, and lost gear.

Flight Agenda and Convenience Subtleties: Have computerized and actual duplicates of your flight tickets and lodging reservations.

Driver's Permit and ID: On the off chance that you intend to lease a vehicle, have your driver's permit. Likewise, convey a copy of your visa as a reinforcement ID.

Gadgets and Embellishments
Power Connector: Barbados utilizes the Sort An and Type B plugs. Bring the fitting power connector if necessary.

Cell Phone and Charger: Guarantee your telephone is opened and consider buying a neighborhood SIM card for reasonable information and call rates.

Camera and Extras: Catch the excellence of Barbados with your camera or cell phone. Remember spare memory cards and chargers.

Wellbeing and Medical aid
Professionally prescribed Meds: In the event that you take any physician endorsed meds, guarantee you have a satisfactory stockpile.

Fundamental Emergency treatment Unit: Pack basics like cement wraps, pain killers, clean wipes, and any private drugs.

Bug Repellent: Mosquitoes can be troublesome. Bring a decent quality bug repellent.

Recommended Things to Purchase in Barbados
Rum: Barbados is known for its excellent rum. Get a container of Mount Gay or other neighborhood brands as a trinket.

Specialties and Fine art: Barbados has a rich imaginative legacy. Search for handcrafted artworks, artistic creations, or stoneware as extraordinary gifts.

Bajan Hot Sauce: The island is popular for its hot sauces. Bring back a Bajan hot sauce to enliven your dinners.

Neighborhood Gems: Barbados offers lovely carefully assembled adornments produced using coral, shells, and valuable metals.

Aloe Vera Items: Alleviate your sun-uncovered skin with privately made aloe vera items.

Barbadian Design: Investigate the nearby business sectors for popular beachwear, dresses, and frill with a Barbadian style.

Barbados is a tropical heaven ready to be investigated. By following this fundamental pressing aide and taking into account the recommended things to purchase, you'll be good to go for an extraordinary excursion to this lovely island. Make sure to pack light, remain safe, and embrace the laid-back Bajan lifestyle. Partake in your excursion!

Chapter 2

Visa and Entry Requirements
Visa and Entry Requirements in Barbados:
Custom Recommendations and Visa Application.

Barbados, a captivating island country settled in the Caribbean, is a fantasy objective for voyagers looking for sun, ocean, and sand. From its dazzling sea shores to lively culture, Barbados brings a lot to the table. In any case, before you leave on your excursion to this tropical heaven, it's fundamental to grasp the visa and passage prerequisites, as well as certain traditions proposals that will make your outing smooth and pleasant.

Visa and Passage Necessities

Sans visa Section: Barbados stretches out a warm greeting to voyagers from numerous nations, offering sans visa passage for short stays. Residents of the US, Canada, the Unified Realm, and most European Association nations can visit Barbados for as long as a half year without a visa. Nonetheless, the particular term of stay allowed can shift by ethnicity, so it's essential to check the Barbados Movement Division's site for the most recent data.

Visa-Required Section: For the people who don't fit the bill for without visa passage, getting a visa is fundamental prior to venturing out to Barbados. It is fitting to apply for a visa well ahead of time to guarantee a smooth passage into the country. Barbados offers a few kinds of visas, like traveler, business, understudy, and travel visas. The expected documentation and handling times might fluctuate relying upon the kind of visa, so reaching the closest Barbadian international safe haven or department for explicit guidance is significant.

Custom Suggestions

Travel Protection: It is energetically prescribed to buy thorough travel protection that covers health related crises, trip undoings, and other unanticipated circumstances. This will give you inner serenity during your visit.

Substantial Identification: Guarantee your visa is legitimate for no less than a half year past your planned flight date from Barbados. It's likewise really smart to make copies of your identification and store them independently in the event of misfortune or burglary.

Money: The authority cash in Barbados is the Barbadian Dollar (BBD). It's smart to have some neighborhood cash close by for little costs, however Visas are broadly acknowledged. You can trade cash at banks and money trade workplaces.

Immunizations: Check with your medical services supplier or travel center for any prescribed inoculations prior to going to Barbados. While there are no particular immunization prerequisites, remaining refreshed on your standard vaccines is fundamental.

Customs Guidelines: Get to know Barbados' traditions guidelines, which remember limitations for the import of specific things like guns, controlled medications, and leafy foods. Inability to agree with these guidelines might bring about fines or seizure of products.

Takeoff Duty: Know that Barbados has a flight charge, which is ordinarily remembered for the cost of your carrier ticket. Be that as it may, it's consistently really smart to twofold check with your carrier to stay away from any amazements at the air terminal.

Regard Neighborhood Customs: Barbadians are known for their warm neighborliness and agreeable nature. Regarding their neighborhood customs and traditions is fundamental. Dress unassumingly while visiting strict destinations, and consistently request authorization prior to taking photographs of local people.

Environment: Barbados partakes in a heat and humidity, and that implies it's warm and bright consistently. The pinnacle traveler season is during the dry season, from December to April, when the weather conditions is charming and precipitation is insignificant. The wet season, from June to November, sees higher stickiness and the chance of downpour, but on the other hand it's an extraordinary opportunity to track down bargains on facilities.

Convenience: Barbados offers an extensive variety of convenience choices to suit each spending plan.

You can find extravagance resorts, shop lodgings, beguiling guesthouses, and get-away rentals. The western and southern coasts are known for their upscale retreats, while the east coast offers a more rough and regular experience.

Food: Barbadian cooking, frequently alluded to as "Bajan," is a brilliant mix of African, Caribbean, and English impacts. Try not to miss attempting neighborhood claims to fame like flying fish and cou, macaroni pie, and seared plantains. Partake in a sample of rum punch, the public beverage, and investigate the island's road food sellers for delightful treats.

Exercises: Barbados offers many exercises for explorers. You can loosen up on its flawless sea shores, go swimming or scuba making a plunge clear waters overflowing with marine life, or even take a shot at water sports like windsurfing and kitesurfing. The island likewise has a lively expressions and music scene, with different celebrations and occasions over time.

Verifiable Locales: History lovers will track down a lot to investigate, including destinations like St.

Nicholas Nunnery, a notable manor house, and Bridgetown, Barbados' capital, which is an UNESCO World Legacy Site. The island additionally has galleries that feature its rich legacy.

Untamed life: Barbados is home to various natural life, including green and hawksbill ocean turtles. You can join directed visits to observe turtle settling and bring forth, a striking and eco-accommodating experience. The island is additionally known for its outlandish birdlife and offers open doors for birdwatching.

Celebrations: Barbados has a scope of brilliant celebrations and occasions over time. Crop Over, the island's greatest celebration, happens from June to August and highlights marches, music, and a lot of neighborhood food. If you have any desire to submerge yourself in Barbadian culture, think about timing your visit to harmonize with one of these celebrations.

Transportation: Getting around Barbados is moderately simple. The island has an advanced street organization, and you can lease a vehicle, take cabs, or utilize the public transport framework. On the other hand, consider investigating the island's coasts and picturesque perspectives by taking a ride on the grand railroad.

Security: Barbados is for the most part thought to be a protected objective for sightseers. Like some other spot, it's fundamental for avoid potential risk, for example, defending your assets and keeping away from dim regions around evening time. Be aware of the sea's flows while swimming, and observe any posted wellbeing rules.

Nearby Manners: While Barbadians are well disposed and inviting, welcoming individuals with a cordial "good day" or "good evening." Tipping is standard, and it's generally expected to leave a 10-15% tip at restaurants is pleasant." While eating with local people, it's a pleasant motion to bring a little gift, similar to a crate of chocolates.

Barbados is a delightful objective with a rich social legacy and staggering regular scenes. Figuring out the visa and section prerequisites, as well as sticking to customs proposals, will guarantee a problem free and charming visit to this Caribbean jewel. Thus, prepare, pack your sunscreen, and prepare to encounter the wizardry of Barbados.

Dos:

1. Do Regard Nearby Traditions:

Barbados has a rich social legacy, and it's critical to be conscious of nearby traditions and customs. This incorporates being considerate and amicable to local people and taking part in nearby occasions and celebrations.

2. Do Attempt Nearby Cooking:

Barbados is renowned for its heavenly food. Try not to pass up on the chance to attempt Bajan dishes like flying fish, cou, and macaroni pie. Visit nearby cafés and attempt road nourishment for a bona fide culinary experience.

3. Do Investigate the Sea shores:

Barbados flaunts shocking sea shores with clear blue waters. Invest energy at famous spots like Crane Ocean side, Carlisle Inlet, and Accra Ocean side. Swimming and water sports are famous exercises along the coast.

4. Do Take part in Water Exercises:

Barbados offers fabulous open doors for scuba plunging, swimming, and water sports. Investigate the energetic marine life, coral reefs, and wrecks. Remember to swim with the ocean turtles at Turtle Ocean side.

5. Do Visit Notable Destinations:

Investigate the island's set of experiences by visiting places like St. Nicholas Convent, George Washington House, and Bridgetown's UNESCO-recorded memorable region. These destinations offer a brief look into Barbados' pilgrim past.

6. Do Partake in the Nightlife:

Barbados wakes up around evening time with dynamic nightlife scenes. Appreciate nearby music, dance, and attempt the island's well known rum punch. Well known nightlife regions incorporate St. Lawrence Hole and Holetown.

7. Do Practice Sun Wellbeing:

Barbados has a heat and humidity, so consistently use sunscreen, wear a cap, and remain hydrated to shield yourself from the solid Caribbean sun. Burn from the sun is unpleasant!

8. Do Visit Nearby Business sectors:

Investigate the beautiful business sectors like Cheapside Market in Bridgetown and Oistins Fish Fry, where you can purchase neighborhood makes, new produce, and experience the energetic air of a Bajan market.

9. Do Find out about Cricket:

Cricket is a lifestyle in Barbados. Regardless of whether you're not a fan, attempt to get a cricket match, or visit the Kensington Oval, one of the world's most well known cricket grounds.

10. Do Regard the Regular Excellence:

- Barbados is honored with rich scenes and regular marvels. Appreciate climbs in places like Welchman Lobby Gorge and investigate the island's caverns, however consistently regard the climate and follow neighborhood guidelines.

11. Do Utilize Nearby Transportation:

- Think about utilizing the nearby open transportation, similar to ZR vans and yellow transports. It's a reasonable method for getting around the island and experience the neighborhood lifestyle.

Don'ts:

1. Remember to deferentially Dress:

While Barbados has a casual climate, it's critical to dress unobtrusively while visiting strict locales or government structures. Swimwear is appropriate just at the ocean side.
2. Try not to Litter:

Keep the island wonderful by discarding your rubbish appropriately. Littering isn't simply insolent yet additionally destructive to the climate and marine life.
3. Try not to Contact the Natural life:

Barbados is home to exceptional untamed life, including ocean turtles. While it's energizing to see them, never upset or contact them. Maintain a conscious separation and keep rules set by neighborhood protection endeavors.
4. Try not to Misjudge the Traffic:

Barbados has left-hand driving, which might be new to some. Be mindful while driving, and recollect that the island's streets can be thin and winding.

5. Try not to Be Discourteous or Forceful:

Be well mannered and obliging to local people. Forceful way of behaving or rude remarks can demolish your experience and mischief the standing of travelers.

6. Try not to Revel in Liquor:

While partaking in Barbados' renowned rum is an unquestionable necessity, don't indulge. Extreme drinking can prompt dangerous circumstances and unfortunate direction.

7. Try not to Overlook Wellbeing Safety measures:

Barbados is by and large protected, yet like any objective, it's crucial for stay mindful of your environmental factors, secure your things, and keep away from unsafe regions, particularly around evening time.

8. Try not to Wrangle Forcefully:
- While bartering is normal in certain regions of the planet, it's anything but a standard practice in

Barbados. Be aware while arranging costs, particularly in shops and markets.

9. Try not to Participate in Criminal operations:
- Taking part in unlawful medication related exercises can bring about extreme punishments in Barbados. Complying with the neighborhood regulations and regulations is fundamental.

10. Remember Travel Protection:
- It's consistently smart to have travel protection that covers unforeseen circumstances like health related crises, trip scratch-offs, and lost possessions. Try not to not accept anything will turn out badly.

11. Try not to Be Inefficient with Water:
- Barbados can encounter water deficiencies, particularly during the dry season. Be aware of water utilization, and stay away from inordinate water wastage, for example, leaving taps running pointlessly.

12. Try not to Overlook Tropical storm Season:
- Barbados is in the storm belt, and typhoon season regularly runs from June to November. Know about the weather patterns during your visit and heed

nearby specialists' guidance in the event of a tropical storm danger.

By following these Rules and regulations, you'll have an extraordinary and differential involvement with Barbados, submerging yourself in the excellence of the island and its warm, inviting society.

Chapter 3

Safety Requirements Providing a Safe and Enjoyable Visit: Barbados Safety Requirements

While arranging an outing to the charming island of Barbados, guaranteeing your security and prosperity is of foremost significance. To make your visit both protected and agreeable, it's fundamental to know about the particular wellbeing prerequisites set up on this wonderful Caribbean island.

Coronavirus Conventions:
Starting around my last information update in January 2022, Barbados had executed severe Coronavirus wellbeing measures. These could incorporate veil wearing out in the open spaces, social separating, and quarantine or testing prerequisites for showing up sightseers. Make certain to actually take a look at the most modern tourism warnings and guidelines from nearby specialists and worldwide associations.

Travel Protection:

It is energetically prescribed to have thorough travel protection that covers health related crises, trip retractions, and other unexpected conditions. This guarantees you have monetary security if there should arise an occurrence of surprising occasions.

Street Wellbeing:
Assuming you intend to lease a vehicle, recall that Barbados follows left-hand driving. Submit to nearby transit regulations and be mindful on winding seaside streets. Safety belts are required, and speed limits are authorized.

Ocean side Wellbeing:
Barbados flaunts shocking sea shores, yet it's essential to know about sea conditions. Focus on banner admonitions, for example, warnings demonstrating perilous surf. Continuously swim inside assigned regions and regard lifeguard directions.

Water Exercises:
Barbados offers a variety of water sports and exercises. While participating in swimming, scuba plunging, or other water undertakings, guarantee

you pick legitimate administrators with confirmed teachers. Security gear ought to be in great shape.

Sun Assurance:
The Caribbean sun can be extreme. Shield yourself from sun related burn by wearing sunscreen, caps, and shades. Remain hydrated, particularly while participating in outside exercises.

Nearby Regulations and Customs:
Find out more about Barbados' regulations and customs. The belonging and utilization of specific substances are unlawful, and public nakedness is restricted. Regard nearby customs and the amicable, neighborly nature of the Barbadian public.

Food and Water:
While Barbados for the most part has safe food and water principles, it's wise to be wary, particularly on the off chance that you have a delicate stomach. Stick to filtered water and eat at legitimate foundations.

Bug Insurance:
Barbados has its portion of bugs, including mosquitoes. To keep away from bug borne illnesses,

use bug repellent, particularly during day break and sunset.

Crisis Contacts:
Save neighborhood crisis numbers and the contact data of your government office or department in the event that you really want help.

All in all, Barbados is a wonderful objective, known for its staggering sea shores, lively culture, and warm neighborliness. By monitoring and sticking to these security necessities, you can guarantee a protected and charming visit, permitting you to relish the marvels of this Caribbean jewel completely. Remember that security guidelines might change over the long haul, so consistently check for the latest data prior to voyaging.

Climate Mindfulness:
Barbados encounters a heat and humidity, and that implies intermittent precipitation and the chance of typhoons during the storm season (commonly June to November). Be aware of weather conditions conjectures and any alerts, particularly assuming that you intend to visit during these months.

Medical care Offices:

Barbados has deeply grounded clinical offices and clinics, however it's as yet essential to have head out protection to cover likely clinical costs. Guarantee you approach a rundown of neighboring clinical focuses and drug stores for good measure.

Cash and Installments:

The authority cash in Barbados is the Barbadian Dollar (BBD), yet the U.S. dollar is generally acknowledged. Charge cards are likewise normally utilized, however it's prudent to have some neighborhood cash for little buys and while making a trip to additional distant regions.

Language:

English is the authority language of Barbados. You'll experience no difficulty speaking with local people, and street signs and different guidelines are in English.

Culture and Decorum:

Barbados has a rich social legacy, and it's fundamental to be conscious of nearby traditions and customs. While visiting strict destinations, covering your shoulders and it is by and large appreciated to wear humble apparel. Regard for older folks and graciousness in connections are profoundly esteemed.

Time Region:
Barbados is on Atlantic Standard Time (AST), which is GMT-4. Know about the time contrast on the off chance that you're going from an alternate time region.

Convenience Decisions:
Barbados offers an extensive variety of convenience choices, from extravagance resorts to spending plan cordial lodgings and get-away rentals. It's wise to book your visit ahead of time, particularly during top vacationer seasons.

Ecological Preservation:
Barbados is home to a novel and delicate environment. Regard neighborhood endeavors to safeguard the climate. Try not to step on coral reefs, don't litter, and partake in eco-accommodating visits and exercises to limit your effect on the climate.

Appreciate Neighborhood Food:

Barbados is prestigious for its flavorful cooking, including dishes like flying fish and cou, as well as different fish choices. Make certain to attempt neighborhood indulgences at legitimate cafés and food stands, and remember to enjoy rum, which is an indispensable piece of Barbadian culture.

Interface with Local people:
One of the most remunerating parts of venturing out to Barbados is the chance to draw in with the well disposed and inviting local people. Find out about their lifestyle, customs, and history, which can incredibly advance your movement experience.

Barbados, with its flawless sea shores, energetic culture, and warm individuals, offers an extraordinary travel insight. By embracing these security necessities and social contemplations, you can make enduring recollections while guaranteeing your prosperity during your visit to this tropical heaven. Continuously stay informed about the recent tourism warnings and guidelines to take advantage of your excursion.

<u>Chapter 4</u>

Money and Budgeting for an Affordable Vacation in Barbados: A Comprehensive Guide to Saving and Targeted Budgeting

Longing for a get-away in the shocking island heaven of Barbados? With its perfect sea shores, energetic culture, and scrumptious food, it's no big surprise why Barbados is a sought-after objective. Be that as it may, a remarkable Barbadian escape doesn't need to burn through every last cent. This thorough aide will assist you with arranging a financial plan accommodating excursion to Barbados without settling for less on your movement experience.

Segment 1: Setting Your Financial plan

1.1 Decide Your All out Financial plan:

Compute your complete financial plan for the excursion, including airfare, convenience, food, exercises, and incidental costs.
1.2 Focus on Your Costs:

Conclude what parts of your outing are generally vital to you, whether it's investigating the neighborhood culture, appreciating water sports, or feasting at upscale eateries.

1.3 Make an Everyday Recompense:

Partition your complete spending plan by the quantity of days you intend to spend in Barbados to decide your everyday stipend.

Segment 2: Putting something aside for Your Outing

2.1 Make a Committed Investment account:

Open a different bank account explicitly for your Barbados get-away to keep your assets separate from your standard costs.

2.2 Cut Pointless Costs:

Audit your month to month spending and cut back on trivial things, for example, eating out or amusement.

2.3 Set Up a Programmed Move:

Mechanize your investment funds by setting up customary exchanges from your primary record to your excursion reserve.

2.4 Side gigs and Additional Pay:

Consider taking on temporary work or independent chances to support your get-away asset.

Segment 3: Reasonable Convenience

3.1 Select Guesthouses or Inns:

Guesthouses and inns can be fundamentally less expensive than extravagance resorts, and they offer an opportunity to interface with local people and different explorers.

3.2 Excursion Rentals:

Investigate excursion rental stages like Airbnb for spending plan cordial and comfortable facilities.

3.3 Timing is Vital:

Go during the off-top season to get lower rates for facilities.

Segment 4: Eating on a Tight spending plan

4.1 Road Food and Neighborhood Diners:

Embrace neighborhood cooking by attempting road food and eating at nearby eateries, which are in many cases more reasonable and true.

4.2 Self-Providing food:

Think about booking facilities with kitchen offices to set up your feasts and save money on eating costs.

Area 5: Transportation Tips

5.1 Utilize Public Vehicle:

Barbados has a dependable public transport framework, which is a lot less expensive than leasing a vehicle or utilizing taxis.

5.2 Walk and Bicycle:

Save money on transportation costs by strolling or leasing a bike for brief excursions.

Area 6: Reasonable Exercises

6.1 Free and Minimal expense Attractions:

Barbados offers a lot of regular magnificence and free attractions, including wonderful sea shores, stops, and climbing trails.

6.2 Gathering Limits and Passes:

Search for bunch limits on exercises and consider buying fascination passes for packaged investment funds.
Segment 7: Various Investment funds

7.1 Cash Trade:

Examination and find the best rates for cash trade to stay away from pointless charges.
7.2 Travel Protection:

While it might appear as though an extra cost, travel protection can set aside you cash if there should arise an occurrence of unanticipated occasions.

Arranging a reasonable excursion in Barbados is not at all impossible with the right planning and saving techniques. By setting an unmistakable financial plan, saving industriously, and settling on savvy decisions in regards to convenience, feasting, transportation, and exercises, you can encounter the excellence and culture of Barbados without stressing your funds. Your fantasy excursion in heaven is reachable, and this complete aide can assist you with making it a reality.

Segment 2: Putting something aside for Your Excursion:

2.1 Make a Committed Bank account: Having a different investment account for your excursion fills a few needs. It, right off the bat, intellectually isolates your excursion assets from regular costs, making it less enticing to dunk into your investment funds. Besides, you can without much of a stretch keep tabs on your development toward your investment funds objective. Search for a record with no or low charges to augment your investment funds.

2.4 Second jobs and Additional Pay: Procuring additional pay can altogether help your get-away asset. Consider independent work, selling things you never again need, or taking on seasonal positions. This additional pay can be coordinated straight into your devoted investment account.

Area 3: Reasonable Convenience:

3.3 Timing is Vital: Barbados, in the same way as other travel objections, has top and off-top seasons. To save money on convenience costs, plan your excursion during the off-top season when costs for housing are lower. Nonetheless, make certain to investigate the climate and nearby occasions, so you can in any case partake in your excursion without limit.

Segment 4: Eating on a Tight spending plan:

4.1 Road Food and Neighborhood Restaurants: One of the delights of voyaging is encountering nearby cooking. Barbados is no exemption, with flavorful road food and reasonable neighborhood cafés. Attempt customary Bajan dishes like flying fish and cou or appreciate rotis from road merchants. This sets aside cash as well as permits you to drench yourself in the neighborhood culture.

Segment 5: Transportation Tips:

5.2 Walk and Bicycle: Barbados is a somewhat little island, and numerous attractions are inside strolling or trekking distance. This saves money on transportation costs as well as permits you to investigate at a more loosened up pace, taking in the beautiful magnificence at your relaxation.

Area 6: Reasonable Exercises:

6.1 Free and Minimal expense Attractions: Barbados is known for its shocking sea shores, and best of all, getting a charge out of them is normally free. You can likewise investigate nature holds and climbing trails with practically no confirmation expenses. Drawing in with the island's regular magnificence can be similarly pretty much as remunerating as costly exercises.

6.2 Gathering Limits and Passes: If there are paid exercises you would rather not miss, consider searching for bunch limits or buying fascination passes that pack different encounters together. This can set aside you cash while as yet permitting you to partake in the island's way of life and history.

Segment 7: Random Investment funds:

7.1 Cash Trade: Make a point to research and look at rates for money trade. Utilizing a nearby ATM to pull out cash in the neighborhood money can frequently give a superior conversion standard contrasted with air terminal or inn trade administrations, which commonly have higher expenses.

7.2 Travel Protection: Putting resources into movement protection for your outing to Barbados is insightful. While it might appear as though an extra expense, it can give true serenity if there should arise an occurrence of surprising occasions like flight scratch-offs, health related crises, or lost gear. Having the right inclusion can set aside you cash over the long haul.

Arranging a reasonable excursion in Barbados is not outside the realm of possibilities with the right planning and saving techniques. By setting a reasonable spending plan, saving constantly, and settling on savvy decisions in regards to convenience, eating, transportation, and exercises, you can encounter the excellence and culture of Barbados without stressing your funds. Your fantasy excursion in heaven is reachable, and this exhaustive aide can assist you with making it a reality.

Chapter 5

Arriving in Barbados

Arriving in Barbados offers a delightful experience filled with warm hospitality, stunning landscapes, and a vibrant culture. To make the most of your trip, it's crucial to plan your arrival carefully. Here's a detailed guide to help you navigate through your arrival, from choosing the best and safest flight option to exploring friendly neighborhoods:

1. Choosing the Best and Safest Flight Option:

Flight Selection: Barbados is served by Grantley Adams International Airport (BGI), located on the southern coast of the island. When selecting your flight, consider airlines with a strong safety track record and good customer reviews. Major carriers like American Airlines, British Airways, and Virgin Atlantic often offer reliable service to Barbados.

Direct Flights: Opt for direct flights if available from your departure location. This reduces layovers and minimizes the risk of disruptions.

COVID-19 Precautions: Check the latest COVID-19 travel regulations and ensure compliance with entry requirements. It's essential to stay informed about any testing or quarantine measures in place.

2. Navigating Through the Airport:

Immigration and Customs: Be prepared for the immigration and customs process. Ensure you have all necessary documents, including your passport, visa (if required), and any health declarations.

Transportation: After clearing customs, you can choose from various transportation options to get to your hotel or accommodation. Taxis, airport shuttles, and car rentals are readily available.

3. Booking a Hotel Near the Airport:

Pros of Airport Hotels: Staying near the airport can be convenient, especially if you have a late arrival or early departure. Some popular airport hotels in Barbados include The Crane Resort, Hilton Barbados Resort, and Courtyard by Marriott Bridgetown.

Alternative Accommodation: If you prefer to be closer to the beach or explore other parts of the island, there are numerous accommodations in different neighborhoods. The South Coast, West Coast, and Christ Church are popular areas for visitors.

4. Exploring Friendly Neighborhoods:

South Coast: The South Coast of Barbados, around St. Lawrence Gap, is known for its lively atmosphere, with numerous restaurants, bars, and nightclubs. It's a great choice for those looking for a vibrant and social scene.

West Coast: The West Coast, including areas like Holetown and Speightstown, offers a more tranquil and upscale experience. You'll find luxurious resorts, beautiful beaches, and fine dining options here.

Christ Church: The Christ Church area, home to the popular Oistins Fish Fry, is a great place to experience local culture and enjoy fresh seafood. The area is known for its relaxed and friendly vibe.

Safety: Barbados is generally a safe destination for travelers. However, it's always advisable to take standard precautions such as safeguarding your belongings and avoiding poorly lit or isolated areas at night.

5. Getting Around Barbados:

Public Transportation: Barbados offers an efficient and affordable public transportation system. The government-operated buses and shared minivans, known as "ZR Vans," can take you to various parts of the island. Be sure to have small change for bus fares.

Renting a Car: Renting a car is a popular choice for those who want more freedom and flexibility in exploring the island. Remember that Barbados follows left-hand driving.

Taxis: Taxis are widely available, and the fares are regulated by the government. Make sure to confirm the fare before starting your journey.

6. Must-See Attractions:

Beaches: Barbados is renowned for its beautiful beaches. Don't miss out on visiting famous ones like Crane Beach, Miami Beach, and the calm waters of Carlisle Bay.

Historical Sites: Explore the island's history at attractions like St. Nicholas Abbey, Barbados Museum, and George Washington House.

Natural Beauty: Discover the natural beauty of Barbados by visiting Hunte's Gardens, Harrison's Cave, and Welchman Hall Gully.

Culinary Delights: Barbados offers a variety of delicious dishes. Try the local specialty, flying fish, at Oistins Fish Fry, and savor Bajan cuisine at restaurants like Champers and The Cliff.

7. Local Culture and Festivals:

Crop Over Festival: If you're visiting during the summer, the Crop Over Festival is a cultural highlight with colorful parades, music, and dancing.

Local Markets: Explore local markets like Cheapside Market and Brighton Farmers Market to experience Barbadian culture and find unique souvenirs.

Music and Dance: Barbados is known for its vibrant music scene, with reggae, soca, and calypso playing a significant role in the culture. Don't miss the opportunity to enjoy live music at local bars and clubs.

8. Health and Safety Tips:

Health Precautions: Ensure that you have comprehensive travel insurance and consider purchasing medical coverage. Stay hydrated, use sunscreen, and be cautious of the strong Caribbean sun.

Water: Stick to bottled water for drinking and brushing your teeth, as tap water is safe but might have a different taste.

Emergency Numbers: Familiarize yourself with emergency numbers, including the local police, ambulance, and fire department.

Chapter 6

Transportation Options in Barbados: Budgeting for Car Rental and owning one's Car on Tour.

While visiting Barbados, transportation is a vital thought for vacationers. The island offers an assortment of transportation choices, each with its own benefits and downsides. Two famous decisions for explorers are vehicle rental and possessing a vehicle as long as necessary. In this nitty gritty substance, we'll investigate the upsides and downsides of the two choices and give bits of knowledge into planning to each.

Vehicle Rental in Barbados:

Experts:

Adaptability: Leasing a vehicle in Barbados offers you the opportunity to investigate the island at your own speed. You can visit famous vacation spots, remote sea shores, and unexpected, yet invaluable treasures without being confined by open transportation plans.

Comfort: Rental vehicles are promptly accessible at the Grantley Adams Worldwide Air terminal and various areas across the island. You can look over an assortment of vehicle types to suit your requirements and inclinations.

Protection: You can partake in your excursion with your gathering in a private and agreeable climate. This choice is great for families, couples, or gatherings of companions who need to keep up with their own space.

No Possession Expenses: You won't have to stress over vehicle upkeep, protection, or fuel costs. It's a problem free choice for vacationers.

Cons:

Cost: Vehicle rental in Barbados can be generally costly, particularly during the high vacationer season. Costs change in light of the sort of vehicle and the rental term.

Driving Difficulties: Barbados observes English driving guidelines, and that implies driving on the left half of the street. For guests from nations with right-hand driving, this change can challenge.

Stopping: Tracking down stopping, particularly in Bridgetown or close to well known attractions, can be a test. You could need to pay for stopping in certain areas.

Possessing Your Vehicle on Visit:

Masters:

Cost Reserve funds: While buying a vehicle might appear as though a huge speculation, it tends to be a practical choice for longer stays. You can exchange the vehicle toward the finish of your excursion.

Driving Experience: Claiming a vehicle permits you to become accustomed to Barbados' driving guidelines and streets, making it more straightforward to explore.

Personalization: You have unlimited authority over your vehicle, including its support, tidiness, and alterations.

Cons:

Forthright Costs: Purchasing a vehicle, even a pre-owned one, can be costly. You'll likewise have to think about protection, enrollment, and support costs.

Exchanging Bothers: Selling the vehicle toward the finish of your excursion can be tedious and may not necessarily in every case ensure a full profit from your speculation.

Driving on the Left: In the event that you're not acquainted with left-side driving, it tends to be scaring, and you could take more time to adjust.

Leaving Issues: Like rental vehicles, finding parking spots in well known regions can be a test.

Planning for Vehicle Rental versus Claiming a Vehicle:

Vehicle Rental Financial plan: To spending plan for vehicle rental, consider the span of your visit and the sort of vehicle you want. Costs can go from $40 to $150 each day. Try to figure fuel costs and any extra protection you might need to buy.

Possessing a Vehicle Financial plan: For buying a vehicle, research the pre-owned vehicle market and think about both forthright and continuous costs. A trade-in vehicle might cost somewhere in the range of $3,000 to $10,000. Protection expenses can change in light of the vehicle and your driving history.

Extra Expenses: notwithstanding the base rental rate, know about expected additional charges, for example, air terminal pickup charges, fuel, GPS rental, kid vehicle seats, and any protection updates. Peruse the tenant contract cautiously to grasp these expenses.

Driving Permit Prerequisites: Barbados acknowledges global driving grants (IDPs), yet you might have to convey your unique driver's permit from your nation of origin too. Check the particular prerequisites before you travel.

Age Limitations: Vehicle rental organizations frequently have age limitations for drivers. Some might expect drivers to be no less than 25 years of age, and there may be extra charges for drivers under a particular age, like 21.

Booking Ahead of time: To get the best rates and accessibility, it's fitting to book your rental vehicle ahead of time, particularly during the high season (December to April).

Possessing Your Vehicle on Visit:

Vehicle Examination: Prior to buying a trade-in vehicle in Barbados, have it completely reviewed by a confided in technician. Guarantee that the vehicle is in great shape and meets your wellbeing prerequisites.

Protection Contemplations: While safeguarding your vehicle, comprehend the inclusion choices accessible. Exhaustive protection gives the most assurance, yet it very well may be more costly. Obligation inclusion is compulsory in Barbados.

Lawful Documentation: Guarantee that you have all the essential legitimate documentation while buying a vehicle, including the bill of offer, move of possession structures, and verification of protection.

Exchanging the Vehicle: In the event that you intend to sell the vehicle prior to leaving Barbados, you might have to explore the nearby market and arrange the selling cost. Remember that the resale worth of your vehicle can vacillate contingent upon its make, model, and condition.

Street Conditions: Barbados has a very much kept up with street organization, however be ready for limited, winding streets and infrequent potholes. A few regions might have steep grades.

At last, the choice between vehicle rental and possessing your vehicle in Barbados will rely upon your own inclinations, spending plan, and the particular prerequisites of your excursion. The two choices can give an astounding method for investigating the island and take advantage of your excursion. It's vital for prepare, investigate as needs be, and know about the related expenses and obligations to have a smooth and charming experience while visiting Barbados.

Chapter 7

The Rules Instructions in Barbados:
Laws and Ethics for Visitors

Visiting Barbados is a wonderful experience, but it's essential for travelers to be aware of the rules, instructions, and ethical considerations when exploring this beautiful Caribbean island. Barbados is known for its friendly locals and stunning landscapes, and respecting its laws and ethics is crucial to ensure a harmonious stay.

Respectful Attire: Barbados has a relatively conservative dress code in public places. Visitors are encouraged to cover up when outside of beach areas. Swimwear should be reserved for the beach, and it's important to dress modestly when exploring the towns and villages.

Littering: Barbados takes great pride in its natural beauty, and littering is a serious offense. Make sure to dispose of your trash in designated bins to help keep the island clean.

Drug Laws: The possession and use of illegal drugs are strictly prohibited in Barbados. The penalties for drug-related offenses can be severe, so it's best to stay away from any illegal substances.

Environmental Conservation: Barbados is home to fragile ecosystems, particularly its coral reefs. Visitors are expected to be responsible and avoid damaging the environment, including refraining from touching or standing on coral while snorkeling or diving.

Respect for Local Customs: Be mindful of local customs and traditions. For instance, it's polite to greet with a friendly "Good morning" or "Good afternoon." Additionally, when invited into a Bajan's home, it's customary to bring a small gift as a token of appreciation.

Beach Etiquette: Barbados boasts some of the world's most stunning beaches. Show consideration for other beachgoers by keeping noise levels down, cleaning up after yourself, and refraining from playing loud music.

Driving Laws: If you plan to rent a car, familiarize yourself with the local traffic laws, including driving on the left side of the road. Seatbelts are mandatory, and drinking and driving is strictly prohibited.

Tipping: Tipping is not always included in bills, so it's customary to leave a 10-15% tip for good service in restaurants and for other services.

Respect Religious Sites: Barbados has a rich cultural heritage, and its churches and religious sites are important to the local community. Visitors should be respectful when visiting these places and dress appropriately.

Local Cuisine: Enjoy Barbadian cuisine, but be mindful of where you eat. Street vendors can offer delicious food, but ensure that they maintain proper hygiene standards to avoid foodborne illnesses.

Public Behavior: Barbados is known for its friendly and welcoming atmosphere. Treat locals with respect and courtesy. Loud, disruptive behavior in public places is generally frowned upon.

Currency and Payment: The official currency of Barbados is the Barbadian Dollar (BBD). Credit cards are widely accepted, but it's a good idea to carry some cash for smaller establishments and markets.

Health and Safety: It's advisable to drink bottled or filtered water to prevent any potential stomach issues. Additionally, it's a good practice to have travel insurance that covers medical emergencies.

Wildlife: Barbados is home to unique wildlife and marine life. Avoid feeding or disturbing animals, as it can disrupt their natural behavior and habitats.

Beach Safety: Pay attention to warning flags on the beaches, which indicate sea conditions. Strong currents can be dangerous, so always adhere to lifeguard instructions and swim in designated areas.

Sun Protection: The Caribbean sun can be intense. Ensure you have adequate sun protection, including sunscreen, sunglasses, and hats to avoid sunburn.

Time Zone: Barbados operates on Atlantic Standard Time (AST), which is 4 hours behind Coordinated

Universal Time (UTC-4). Adjust your schedules accordingly.

Emergency Numbers: Save important contact numbers like the local police, hospital, and embassy in case of any emergencies.

Local Events and Festivals: Embrace the local culture by participating in festivals and events when possible. The Crop Over Festival, for example, is a vibrant celebration of Barbadian culture.

Language: English is the official language in Barbados, and it's widely spoken. Learning a few common Bajan expressions can enhance your interactions with the locals.

Respecting these rules and ethical guidelines not only ensures an enjoyable and trouble-free visit to Barbados but also demonstrates your appreciation for the local culture and environment. By being a responsible and respectful visitor, you can fully immerse yourself in the island's beauty and warm hospitality.

Chapter 8

Barbados Cultural Events and Festivals

Barbados, a picturesque island in the Caribbean, is renowned for its rich cultural heritage and vibrant traditions, celebrated through a myriad of cultural events and festivals throughout the year. These gatherings offer a unique opportunity for both locals and visitors to immerse themselves in the island's history, music, dance, and culinary delights. Here, we delve into the diverse array of cultural events and festivals that make Barbados a hub of celebration and merriment.

Crop Over Festival:
One of the most famous and eagerly awaited cultural events in Barbados is the Crop Over Festival, which typically runs from June to early August. This festival has deep historical roots, originally celebrating the end of the sugar cane harvest, and it has since evolved into a colorful extravaganza of music, dance, and revelry. The festival includes a range of activities, from calypso competitions to

grand costume parades known as "Foreday Morning" and "Grand Kadooment." Revelers adorned in elaborate costumes, dance to the infectious rhythms of soca and calypso music as they make their way through the streets of Bridgetown.

Holetown Festival:

The Holetown Festival, celebrated in February, marks the anniversary of the first English settlement in Barbados in 1627. This event is a showcase of Barbadian heritage and features various activities, including historical reenactments, local craft exhibitions, and lively street fairs. It's a great opportunity to learn about the island's history and enjoy the warm hospitality of the local community.

Oistins Fish Festival:

Barbados has a strong maritime tradition, and the Oistins Fish Festival held over the Easter weekend is a testament to this. Visitors can indulge in an array of delectable seafood dishes and enjoy various competitions and entertainment, such as fish boning and grease pole climbing. It's a true celebration of Barbados' fishing heritage.

Reggae Festival:

For those who are fans of reggae music, Barbados hosts an annual Reggae Festival that brings together international and local reggae artists. This festival usually takes place in April and features a series of concerts, beach parties, and cultural performances, giving visitors the chance to groove to the rhythms of this iconic genre.

Holders Season:

Holders Season is an annual festival that celebrates the arts, with a focus on music, dance, and theater. This festival typically runs from March to April and features performances by local and international artists in a stunning open-air theater. The event is set against the backdrop of the historic Holders House, creating a unique and enchanting atmosphere.

Hoopla:

Hoopla is a family-friendly festival that usually takes place in December. It's a lively event that combines music, dance, and various activities for children. Visitors can enjoy live music performances, food vendors, and entertainment for all ages.

Food and Rum Festival:
For culinary enthusiasts, the Food and Rum Festival held in October is a must-attend event. It offers a delightful culinary experience, showcasing the best of Bajan cuisine and top-quality rum. Renowned local and international chefs prepare delectable dishes, and visitors can also indulge in rum tastings and mixology demonstrations.

Independence Day:
Barbados gained independence from British colonial rule on November 30th, 1966, and every year, the island celebrates this significant milestone with a grand Independence Day parade and other festivities. The day begins with a ceremonial changing of the guard and is followed by a colorful parade featuring marching bands, cultural displays, and vibrant costumes. It's an excellent opportunity to witness national pride and enjoy the lively atmosphere.

Regatta:
Sailing enthusiasts will find the Barbados Regatta, typically held in mid-January, to be an exciting event. The island's clear waters and consistent trade winds provide the perfect conditions for competitive

sailing. The regatta includes a series of yacht races and beach parties, attracting both local and international sailors.

Jazz Festival:
For lovers of smooth tunes and soulful melodies, the Barbados Jazz Festival in January offers a fantastic experience. This event features internationally acclaimed jazz artists who perform at various venues across the island. The setting, often with the backdrop of the Caribbean Sea, creates an intimate and soothing atmosphere for jazz enthusiasts.

Surf Festivals:
Barbados is a renowned destination for surfers, and it hosts several surf competitions and festivals throughout the year. The island's coastline offers excellent waves for all levels of surfers. The Barbados Surf Pro, held in November, is part of the World Surf League and attracts top international surfers. Additionally, the Soup Bowl Surf Festival in Bathsheba is an annual event that celebrates the local surf culture.

Horse Racing:

Horse racing has a long history in Barbados, and the Barbados Turf Club hosts several race meetings throughout the year. The most prestigious of these events is the Sandy Lane Gold Cup, held in March. It's not just a horse race; it's a social and fashion event where attendees don their finest attire and enjoy a day at the races.

Fisherman's Day:
Fisherman's Day is celebrated annually in June and pays tribute to the island's fishing community. The festivities include boat races, fish frying competitions, and cultural displays. It's a unique opportunity to appreciate the contributions of local fishermen to Barbados' culture and cuisine.

These cultural events and festivals in Barbados offer a diverse range of experiences, from music and dance to sports and culinary delights. Whether you're interested in history, adventure, or simply having a good time, Barbados provides ample opportunities to immerse yourself in its rich cultural heritage and vibrant traditions. The island's warm hospitality and infectious enthusiasm make these events even more special, ensuring that your visit to Barbados will be a memorable one.

Chapter 9

Accommodation Options Accommodation Options in Barbados: Budgeting for Rental Homestay and Hotels.

While arranging an excursion to Barbados, it's fundamental to think about your convenience choices and planning to guarantee you have an agreeable and charming stay. Barbados offers various decisions, from financial plan cordial to lavish facilities, permitting you to fit your visit to your inclinations and monetary arrangement.

1. Lodgings:

Barbados brags a wide reach lodgings, going from financial plan well disposed choices to top of the line resorts. By and large, you can find lodgings in the accompanying cost ranges:

Financial plan: $50 - $150 each evening

Mid-Reach: $150 - $300 each evening

Extravagance: $300+ each evening

Financial plan Cordial Lodgings: For those hoping to save money on convenience, you can find agreeable financial plan inns in regions like Bridgetown and St. Lawrence Hole. These choices give essential conveniences and are reasonable for voyagers on a more tight financial plan.

Mid-Reach Lodgings: The mid-range inn choices in Barbados offer more conveniences, like pools, nearby eating, and closeness to the ocean side. You can find large numbers of these in the well known vacationer regions like Holetown and Oistins.

Extravagance Resorts: In the event that you're willing to go overboard, Barbados is home to various top of the line resorts and shop lodgings. These properties frequently incorporate comprehensive bundles, spa administrations, and admittance to private sea shores. The west shore of the island, known as the Platinum Coast, is renowned for extravagance facilities.

2. Rental Homes and Manors:

Barbados is known for its lovely rental homes and manors, which give a more private and extensive housing choice. Costs for rental homes and estates can change broadly founded on the spot, size, and conveniences. Here is an unpleasant breakdown:

Spending plan: $100 - $250 each evening
Mid-Reach: $250 - $500 each evening
Extravagance: $500+ each evening
Spending plan Rentals: There are reasonable rental homes and condos accessible on the island, particularly in calmer regions like Bathsheba and Speightstown. These choices are great for families or gatherings searching for a more long-term visit.

Mid-Reach Rentals: In well known vacationer regions, for example, Christ Church and St. James, you can track down roomy estates and rental homes that offer a blend of solace and worth.

Extravagance Manors: Barbados is renowned for its excessive estates with stunning sea sees. A large number of these properties accompany private pools, individual culinary experts, and selective ocean side access. They are ideally suited for a lavish retreat.

3. Homestays and Guesthouses:

For a more neighborhood and financial plan cordial experience, you can investigate homestays, guesthouses, and overnight boardinghouse choices in Barbados. Costs can go from $50 to $150 each evening, pursuing it a brilliant decision for voyagers who need to drench themselves in the nearby culture.

Homestays and guesthouses offer an opportunity to interface with Barbadian inhabitants, taste bona fide cooking, and get insider tips on the most ideal getaway spots on the island.

4. Comprehensive Hotels:

Barbados has a determination of comprehensive retreats that offer a problem free get-away insight. These retreats ordinarily incorporate convenience, feasts, drinks, and different exercises in the bundle cost. Costs can shift from mid-reach to extravagance, with the Platinum Coast being home to the absolute best choices.

5. Airbnb and Get-away Rental Stages:

Airbnb and other get-away rental stages are likewise well known in Barbados. They offer a great many properties, from ocean front lofts to field houses. Costs can differ, so you can track down choices to suit your spending plan.

6. Condo Rentals:

In the event that you're looking for a more self-providing food experience, loft rentals are an extraordinary decision. You can find condos in different cost ranges, from spending plan to extravagance, in areas like St. Lawrence Hole, Worthing, and Maxwell Coast Street. These are appropriate for voyagers who need to prepare their feasts and have greater adaptability during their visit.

7. Inns:

Barbados likewise has a couple of lodgings that take care of frugal voyagers, especially in Bridgetown. Lodgings offer residence style convenience, going with them a fantastic decision for solo explorers or hikers. Costs normally range from $20 to $40 each evening.

8. Guesthouses and Motels:

The island is dabbed with enchanting guesthouses and motels that offer a comfortable and close stay. These facilities frequently accompany an individual touch and are found in both touristy and off in an unexpected direction regions.

Planning Tips:

Consider going during the off-top season (regularly from June to November) to find lower convenience costs.

Utilize internet booking stages and correlation sites to track down the best arrangements and advancements.

On the off chance that you intend to remain longer, consider arranging a limited rate with the land owner or supervisor.

Search for convenience bundles that incorporate added advantages, for example, air terminal exchanges or visit limits.

Extra Ideas:

While picking convenience, ponder what means quite a bit to you: nearness to the ocean side, nightlife, or a tranquil retreat.

Research the various shores of Barbados: the quiet west coast, ideal for swimming and dusks, and the more tough east coast, ideal for surfing and nature sweethearts.

Remember that a few properties offer free breakfast, which can save money on feasting costs.

Investigate nearby business sectors and diners for reasonable and scrumptious Bajan cooking.

Barbados offers a different scope of convenience choices to take special care of different spending plans and inclinations. Whether you're searching for an ocean front manor, a comfortable guesthouse, or a spending plan cordial inn, you can track down the ideal spot to remain while investigating the shocking scenes and dynamic culture of this Caribbean diamond. Preparing, being adaptable with your movement dates, and using accessible assets will assist you with taking full advantage of your Barbados experience without burning through every last dollar.

Chapter 10

Best Time to Visit Barbados for Perfect Weather And Memorable Experiences.

Barbados, a Caribbean pearl settled in the eastern Caribbean Ocean, is a heaven known for its perfect sea shores, rich social legacy, and lively environment. While arranging the ideal visit to this tropical heaven, timing is everything. To encounter the best climate and make enduring recollections, consider these experiences on the best opportunity to investigate Barbados.

1. Amazing Climate in the High Season:
The best opportunity to visit Barbados is during the high season, which ranges from December to April. During this period, the island encounters charming and unsurprising atmospheric conditions. With temperatures averaging around 80-85°F (27-30°C), you'll delight in the warm, sun-kissed days and serenely cool nights. The exchange winds give a reviving breeze, making it the ideal environment for different open air exercises.

2. Get away from the Stormy Season:

Barbados has a stormy season from June to November, which concurs with typhoon season in the Caribbean. While typhoons are moderately uncommon in Barbados, there's a higher opportunity of weighty precipitation and periodic hurricanes during these months. To stay away from expected disturbances to your excursion designs, arranging your outing outside this period is ideal.

3. Partake in the Celebrations:
In the event that you're searching for a one of a kind social encounter, visiting Barbados during its energetic celebration season is an unquestionable necessity. Crop Over Celebration, praised from May to August, is a fantastic occasion highlighting dynamic processions, nearby music, and scrumptious cooking. The island wakes up with energy, offering a paramount social encounter.

4. Snorkel and Make a plunge Completely clear Waters:
The long stretches of April to October are fantastic for submerged undertakings in Barbados. The perceivability is at its top during these months, making it an ideal time for swimming and scuba jumping. Investigate the beautiful coral reefs,

wrecks, and different marine life that flourish in the completely clear waters.

5. Reserve funds in the Shoulder Season:
For thrifty voyagers, the shoulder season (May and November) is an incredible opportunity to visit. Convenience and flights will generally be more reasonable, and you can in any case appreciate charming climate and the dazzling magnificence of Barbados without the pinnacle season swarms.

6. Embrace the Merry Soul:
In the event that you're attracted to the occasion soul and wish to observe Christmas and New Year's in a tropical heaven, Barbados is the ideal objective. The island is enhanced with happy designs, and different occasions and gatherings make for a genuinely noteworthy Christmas season.

The best opportunity to visit Barbados for wonderful climate and critical encounters is during the high season, from December to April. With its calm environment, social merriments, and open doors for outside undertakings, Barbados is an all year objective, however the high season offers an unrivaled mix of ideal climate and remarkable encounters. Whether you're looking for unwinding on the ocean front, exciting water sports, or social drenching, Barbados makes certain to leave you with enduring recollections of a tropical heaven.

Here is a rundown of some well known traveler objections in Barbados and the best times to visit every one for an ideal encounter:

1. Bridgetown:
Bridgetown, the capital of Barbados, is a clamoring city with noteworthy appeal and dynamic business sectors. The best opportunity to investigate Bridgetown is during the dry season, from December to April, when you can walk around its brilliant roads, visit memorable destinations, and appreciate shopping without the interference of weighty downpours.

2. Oistins:
If you have any desire to encounter the enthusiastic Oistins Fish Fry, head there on a Friday night over time. This social and culinary occasion is a must-visit, offering delectable fish and a vivacious air.

3. Bathsheba:

Bathsheba, situated on the rough east coast, is popular for its striking stone developments and a-list surfing. The best time for surf aficionados to visit is during the Atlantic storm season, from June to November, when the waves are at their generally exciting. For a more quiet encounter, visit during the dry season.

4. Creature Blossom Cavern:

This regular marvel on the northern coast is a spellbinding cavern with staggering ocean sees. It's best investigated during the dry season, from December to April, when the ocean is more quiet and the cavern's pools are more secure for swimming.

5. Hunte's Nursery:

For a rich and quiet organic experience, visit Hunte's Nursery all year. The delightfully finished garden offers a peaceful departure from the intensity, yet the dynamic foliage is especially dazzling during the stormy season when everything is in full blossom.

6. Harrison's Cavern:

Harrison's Cavern is a land miracle, and it's best investigated when the weather conditions is dry and stable. Plan your visit during the high season, from December to April, for the most agreeable and charming cavern visits.

7. St. Nicholas Convent:
This noteworthy ranch house is a well known vacation destination. The best opportunity to visit is during the high season, as the weather conditions is charming, and you can completely partake in the directed visits and the delightful environmental elements.

Recall that Barbados offers a different scope of attractions, from verifiable locales to regular marvels, and the best chance to visit every objective might fluctuate. It's essential to design your schedule in view of your inclinations and the particular elements of every area, considering the climate and any occasional occasions or celebrations that could improve your experience.

Chapter 11
Barbados, Top Tourist Destinations You Must See.

Barbados is a staggering Caribbean island with a rich social legacy and an assortment of traveler objections that offer something for everybody. Here are a portion of the top vacationer locations in Barbados and the remarkable highlights that make every one of them an unquestionable necessity:

Bridgetown - The Capital City:

Bridgetown is the capital city of Barbados and an UNESCO World Legacy site. It's known for its noteworthy frontier engineering, bright roads, and dynamic business sectors. Try not to miss the Parliament Structures and the Nidhe Israel Gathering place, which is perhaps of the most established temple in the Western Half of the globe.
Crane Ocean side - Regular Magnificence:

Crane Ocean side is much of the time thought about quite possibly of the most gorgeous ocean side on the planet. Its novel pink-touched sands, perfectly clear waters, and emotional bluffs make it a must-visit objective. You can likewise remain at the notable Crane Resort, roosted on the bluffs over the ocean side.

Harrison's Cavern - Underground Miracle:

Harrison's Cavern is a characteristic miracle, including a complicated organization of underground caverns and passages. Guests can take directed cable car visits through the cavern framework, wondering about the staggering tapered rocks, stalagmites, and underground cascades.

Creature Bloom Cavern - Land Wonder:

This ocean cave, situated on the northern tip of the island, is named after the brilliant ocean anemones that occupy its pools. The cavern offers stunning sea perspectives and exceptional stone developments, making it a pleasant objective for investigation.

Oistins Fish Fry - Culinary Joy:

Oistins Fish Fry is a week after week occasion where local people and travelers assemble to appreciate Barbadian food, especially new fish. The vivacious environment, music, and heavenly food make it an interesting social encounter.

Barbados Untamed life Hold - Normal Experiences:

This save offers an opportunity to see Barbados' different untamed life very close. You can notice green monkeys, turtles, and different extraordinary birds in a characteristic setting. It's a one of a kind chance to interface with the island's fauna.

St. Nicholas Nunnery - Memorable Ranch:

St. Nicholas Nunnery is a seventeenth century manor house, offering a brief look into Barbados' frontier history. Guests can visit the house, nurseries, and rum refinery, and test their renowned rum.

Barbados Gallery and Authentic Culture - Social Understanding:

This exhibition hall is housed in a previous English military jail and gives a top to bottom gander at Barbados' set of experiences, culture, and legacy. It's a superb spot to find out about the island's past and its kin.

Andromeda Botanic Nurseries - Tropical Heaven:

Situated on the east coast, these nurseries highlight a wide assortment of tropical plants, including orchids and palms. The lavish plant life and serene setting make it a tranquil getaway.

Bathsheba - Surfer's Heaven:

Bathsheba is a rough seaside region on the east coast known for its tremendous stone developments and solid waves. It's a sanctuary for surfers and photographic artists, offering an exceptional difference to the quiet, sandy sea shores tracked down somewhere else on the island.

Mount Gay Rum Refinery - Refinery Visit:

Barbados is popular for its rum, and the Mount Gay Rum Refinery, established in 1703, is the most seasoned rum refinery on the planet. Take a directed visit to find out about the rum-production process and appreciate tastings of their extraordinary items.

Farley Slope Public Park - Grand Excellence:

This public park offers lavish green spaces, strolling trails, and astounding perspectives on the east coast. The focal point is the Farley Slope Extraordinary House, which is presently in ruins yet adds a verifiable touch to the recreation area's normal magnificence.

Welchman Lobby Chasm - Organic Wonder:

Investigate the interesting chasm, an imploded cave framework, loaded up with a lavish professional flowerbed. It's a peaceful spot to see various tropical plants and find out about Barbados' land history.

Post Savannah - Horse Racing Fervor:

On the off chance that you really love horse racing, the Post Savannah is the spot to be. You can encounter the excitement of the races, particularly during the Barbados Gold Cup, a renowned occasion in the Caribbean horse racing schedule.

Sunbury Manor House - Notable Home:

Sunbury Manor House is a wonderfully saved seventeenth century ranch domain. It offers a brief look into the island's set of experiences, with classical decorations, an assortment of carriages, and very much manicured gardens.

Folkestone Marine Park - Swimming Shelter:

Folkestone Marine Park is a safeguarded region that offers magnificent swimming open doors.

Investigate dynamic coral reefs, submerged figures, and a submerged wreck, making it a remarkable encounter for submerged fans.

Barbados Workmanship Display - Creative Articulation:

The Barbados Workmanship Display includes a different assortment of craftsmanship by nearby and worldwide specialists. It's an incredible spot to see the value in the island's imaginative scene and maybe buy a remarkable piece of Barbadian craftsmanship.

Miami Ocean side - Isolated Tranquility:

Miami Ocean side, situated on the southern coast, offers a more isolated and less packed ocean side insight. It's ideal for a calm day of sunbathing, swimming, and picnicking.

St. John's Ward Church - Strict Legacy:

This notable church, roosted on a slope, offers all encompassing perspectives on the island's eastern shoreline. Its Gothic engineering and quiet environmental elements make it a tranquil spot for reflection and photography.

Graeme Lobby Nature Asylum - Avian Heaven:

This safe-haven is a sanctuary for birdwatchers, with different types of fascinating and local birds. The rich scenes and quiet lakes make a tranquil environment for guests to appreciate.

Every one of these locations in Barbados offers a novel encounter, whether it's the normal excellence, verifiable importance, social extravagance, or culinary enjoyments. Investigating these spots will permit you to submerge yourself in the appeal and variety of this Caribbean pearl genuinely.

Chapter 12

Dining and entertainment restaurants in Barbados

Barbados is a lovely island in the Caribbean known for its staggering sea shores, rich culture, and energetic eating and diversion scene. With regards to eating and amusement, Barbados offers a different scope of choices to take care of all preferences and inclinations. Here is a definite outline of feasting and diversion in Barbados:

1. High end Cafés:

Barbados flaunts various high end foundations that offer a mix of neighborhood and worldwide cooking. The Bluff Eatery, eminent for its stupendous beach front setting, offers a menu of new fish and connoisseur dishes. Cin by the Ocean is one more upscale decision, with Mediterranean-motivated dishes and all encompassing ocean sees.

2. Fish Claims to fame:

Given its beach front area, Barbados is popular for its fish. Oistins Fish Fry is a must-visit spot for real

Bajan broiled fish and other fish dishes. Guests can appreciate delightful mahi, flying fish, and lobster, all presented with conventional side dishes like macaroni pie and coleslaw.

3. Nearby Cooking:

Barbados is well known for its special nearby dishes. Guests can attempt cou and flying fish, which is viewed as the public dish. Other Bajan top choices incorporate pepperpot, a sluggish cooked meat stew, and pudding and immerse, a blend of salted pork and steamed yam.

4. Relaxed Eating:

For a more loosened up eating experience, Barbados offers a lot of relaxed choices. The Tides, situated on the west coast, offers a different menu in an enchanting ocean front setting. Bistro Luna, with its Mediterranean-roused menu, is one more fantastic decision for a relaxed at this point charming feasting experience.

5. Nightlife and Diversion:

Barbados has a dynamic nightlife with a lot of choices for diversion. St. Lawrence Hole is a focal point for bars, dance club, and unrecorded music.

Harbor Lights is known for its vivacious ocean front gatherings and shows. The Barbados nightlife scene frequently incorporates reggae and soca music, making it an extraordinary spot to encounter the island's way of life.

6. Rum Refineries:

Barbados is renowned for its rum creation. Guests can investigate rum refineries like Mount Gay, Foursquare, and St. Nicholas Monastery to find out about the set of experiences and creation of this notorious Caribbean soul. These visits frequently end with tastings of different rum assortments.

7. Supper Shows:

A few cafés in Barbados offer supper shows for a total diversion experience. The Estate Theater and Supper Show, for instance, gives a night of top notch food and charming exhibitions going from satire to music.

8. Comprehensive developments:

Barbados has different far-reaching developments and celebrations over time, which frequently incorporate food and amusement. The Yield Over Celebration, held in the late spring, is a lively festival of Bajan culture with music, dance, and culinary joys.

9. Ocean front Feasting:

Numerous cafés in Barbados are arranged on beautiful sea shores. Eating at places like The Solitary Star or The Fish Pot offers delectable food as well as stunning sea sees, making a critical feasting experience.

10. Waterfront Eating:

Numerous cafés in Barbados are found right on the water's edge, giving a heartfelt and beautiful feasting experience. Eateries like The Fish Pot, Earthy colored Sugar, and Lobster Alive proposition burger joints the chance to partake in their dinners with a dazzling sea scenery.

11. Road Food:

For a sample of genuine Bajan road food, guests can investigate the nearby food slows down and road sellers. You'll find top picks like fish cakes, rotis, and tasty seared chicken. The clamoring roads of Bridgetown, Barbados' capital, are an incredible spot to test these enjoyments.

12. Nightfall Travels:

To consolidate feasting and diversion with a beautiful encounter, think about taking a nightfall voyage. These travels frequently incorporate a scrumptious supper while you partake in the delightful Caribbean nightfall. It's an extraordinary method for loosening up and value the island's normal excellence.

13. Ocean side Bars:

Ocean side bars in Barbados are easygoing and fun, offering a casual environment and frequently facilitating unrecorded music occasions. Famous ocean side bars like Bajan Roots and Ju's Ocean side Bar give extraordinary mixed drinks and nearby food right on the sand.

14. Unrecorded Music:

Barbados has an enthusiastic unrecorded music scene, with many bars and cafés highlighting live groups playing reggae, soca, calypso, and jazz. Scenes like Blakey's on the Footpath and The Boatyard frequently have unrecorded music exhibitions.

15. Sports Bars:

If you're a games lover and don't have any desire to miss a game, Barbados has sports bars that broadcast global occasions. These bars serve commonplace bar food and are an incredible spot to loosen up and get your number one games.

16. Wellbeing Cognizant Eating:

For those searching for wellbeing cognizant choices, Barbados has a developing number of cafés offering veggie lover, vegetarian, and sans gluten menus. Easy street Bistro in Holetown is a well known decision for solid and natural dishes.

17. Family-Accommodating Feasting:

Barbados is a family-accommodating objective, and you can find a lot of eateries that take care of families with kids. Many deal kid-accommodating menus and play regions. The Ocean side House and Privateers Bay are brilliant choices for a family feasting experience.

18. Themed Eateries:

A few eateries in Barbados offer special themed feasting encounters. For instance, the Boatyard offers a tomfoolery and lively air with a water park and trampolines for visitors to appreciate.

19. Food Celebrations:

Consistently, Barbados has different food celebrations praising the island's culinary practices. The Food and Rum Celebration, Barbados Chocolate and Cake Celebration, and Holetown Celebration are only a couple of instances of occasions that grandstand neighborhood cooking.

20. Culinary Visits:

For a more vivid encounter, think about taking a culinary visit to investigate the island's business sectors, taste nearby fixings, and even partake in cooking classes to figure out how to plan conventional Bajan dishes.

Barbados offers a different culinary and diversion scene, taking care of a large number of tastes and inclinations. Whether you're looking for top notch food with sea sees, neighborhood Bajan cooking, relaxed ocean front feasts, or energetic nightlife, Barbados has everything, making it a top objective for those hoping to enjoy the flavors and culture of the Caribbean.

Chapter 13

Hidden Gems in Barbados: A Treasure Hunt Through Its Unknown Gems

Barbados, frequently eminent for its dazzling sea shores and extravagant hotels, is a gold mine of unexpected, yet invaluable treasures ready to be found by gutsy voyagers. Past the very much trampled vacationer ways lie less popular fortunes that uncover the island's rich history, energetic culture, and regular magnificence. Leave on an expedition through Barbados to uncover these unexpected, yet invaluable treasures.

Hunte's Nurseries: Settled in the rich inside of the island, Hunte's Nurseries is a tranquil desert garden that feels like its very own universe. Made by horticulturist Anthony Hunte, this unexpected, yet invaluable treasure brags an entrancing assortment tropical plants, wandering pathways, and serene niches. A plant heaven transports you to an alternate domain.

Bathsheba: While numerous guests rush toward the southern coast's flawless sea shores, the tough excellence of Bathsheba on the east coast stays a mystery escape. The emotional stone developments, beating Atlantic waves, and the renowned Soup Bowl surf break make it a safe house for surfers and photographic artists.

Creature Bloom Cavern: Concealed in the northernmost tip of Barbados, the Creature Blossom Cavern is a noteworthy geographical development that offers stunning perspectives on the sea. Investigate the antiquated coral reef, complete with regular stone pools and captivating ocean anemones, referred to locally as "creature blossoms."

St. Nicholas Convent: This notable estate house is an unlikely treasure wealthy in history and engineering magnificence. It's one of just three certified Jacobean houses in the Western Side of the equator. Take a visit to find out about its 350-year-old history, taste on their rum, and investigate the captivating nurseries.

Welchman Lobby Gorge: Adventure into this captivating tropical chasm and be moved to an ancient scene. The lavish vegetation, transcending palm trees, and twittering natural life make a supernatural air. Walk around the wandering ways and you could detect some green monkeys.

Sunbury Estate House: Step back in time at Sunbury Ranch House, a very much saved seventeenth century chateau. It houses a great assortment of collectibles, carriages, and relics, giving a brief look into Barbados' pioneer history.

Barbados Natural life Save: Situated in a mahogany woods, this hold offers a novel chance to get up near native and extraordinary creatures. Watch the green monkeys, turtles, peacocks, and more right at home.

Cherry Tree Slope: Drive along the pleasant Cherry Tree Slope, and you'll be compensated with clearing perspectives on the eastern and northern coasts. It's an optimal spot for a relaxed cookout and probably the best vistas on the island.

Bridgetown's Property Houses: Investigate the bright asset houses in Bridgetown, little wooden designs that are important for Barbados' legacy. They feature the island's energetic engineering and history.

East Coast Excursion: Take a relaxed drive along the twisting streets of the east coast, going through enchanting towns and partaking in the tough waterfront landscape. This less-visited piece of the island offers an alternate point of view of Barbados.

Andromeda Botanic Nurseries: Situated in the town of Bathsheba, this charming professional flowerbed is a demonstration of the island's momentous biodiversity. Walk around the lavish vegetation, find intriguing and outlandish plant species, and respect the energetic blossoms that paint a beautiful scene.

Base Straight: This separated, bow molded ocean side is a secret heaven. Transcending palm trees, limestone precipices, and fine white sand make it an optimal spot for a peaceful break. The normal limestone opening and the turquoise waters make a postcard-commendable scene.

Mount Gay Rum Refinery: For those intrigued by the set of experiences and craft of rum-production, a visit to Mount Gay Refinery is an unquestionable requirement. Find the legacy of Barbados' most popular product, taste different rums, and find out about the refining system.

Post Savannah: Step once more into frontier period Barbados by investigating the noteworthy Post region. Home to noteworthy military structures, race tracks, and historical centers, it's an UNESCO World Legacy Site and a window into the island's past.

Hackleton's Precipice: For a portion of experience and all encompassing perspectives, dare to Hackleton's Bluff, quite possibly of the greatest point on the island. Climb to the culmination, and you'll be compensated with stunning vistas of the west and east drifts, as well as lavish vegetation and, surprisingly, a goliath banyan tree.

Nidhe Israel Gathering place: Find Barbados' Jewish legacy at Nidhe Israel, perhaps of the most seasoned temple in the Western Half of the globe. The contiguous exhibition hall and memorable graveyard offer bits of knowledge into the island's rich social embroidery.

Oistins Fish Market: While Oistins is a notable spot for new fish, the fish market stays a secret fortune for foodies. Test delectable Bajan dishes like seared flying fish, cou, and macaroni pie, ready by neighborhood sellers.

Pico Tenerife: For a remarkable open air experience, climb to Pico Tenerife, the most noteworthy point in Barbados. The compensation for your endeavors incorporates all encompassing perspectives on the island and the encompassing Caribbean Ocean.

Soup Bowl Figure Park: Situated in Bathsheba, this outdoors craftsmanship exhibition highlights models made by neighborhood specialists. The works are motivated by the rough excellence of the east coast and make for an interesting and imaginative quit during your visit.

Speightstown: Frequently eclipsed by Bridgetown, Speightstown is a beguiling, noteworthy town with restricted roads, pioneer engineering, and a dynamic neighborhood scene. Visit Arlington House Exhibition hall and investigate the town's remarkable person.

As you leave on your expedition through Barbados, recollect that these unlikely treasures are a demonstration of the island's variety and the glow of its kin. Past the dazzling sea shores, you'll find a universe of history, culture, and normal ponders that add profundity and wealth to your Barbadian experience. Partake in your experience!

Chapter 14

Souvenir Shopping in Barbados

Souvenir shopping in Barbados can be a delightful experience, as this Caribbean island offers a wide range of unique and locally-made items that are perfect for bringing a piece of the island back home. Whether you're looking for traditional Bajan crafts, artisanal products, or simply a reminder of your time in paradise, Barbados has something for everyone.

What to Buy:

Crafts and Artwork: Barbados is known for its vibrant art scene. Look for local paintings, pottery, and sculptures, often inspired by the island's natural beauty and culture. The works of Barbadian artists are not only beautiful but also a great way to support local talent.

Rum: Barbados is famous for its rum, and you can't leave without a bottle of Mount Gay or Doorly's. The island's rich sugarcane history has made it a hub for rum production. Many distilleries offer tours where you can learn about the process and taste different rums.

Local Food and Spices: Barbadian cuisine is a delightful fusion of flavors. Pick up some Bajan hot sauce, pepper jelly, or seasoning blends to add a taste of the island to your dishes back home. Flying fish is a local delicacy, and you can find it in various forms, including canned or dried for easy transportation.

Jewelry: Handcrafted jewelry is a popular choice, with items made from seashells, coral, and precious stones. You can find elegant pieces as well as more casual, beach-inspired designs.

Clothing and Fabrics: Colorful and breezy clothing, especially beachwear, is widely available. Look for batik fabrics, which are hand-dyed with intricate patterns and often used to create beautiful garments.

Where to Shop:

Oistins Fish Market: Visit Oistins on Friday night for the famous fish fry, and while you're there, explore the market for local crafts, jewelry, and artwork. It's a lively atmosphere with great local food as well.

Pelican Craft Centre: Located in Bridgetown, this center is home to numerous shops selling traditional Bajan crafts and art. It's a great place to find unique souvenirs.

Chattel Village: These clusters of colorful wooden huts scattered across the island house various shops selling local wares, from clothing to crafts. Holetown and St. Lawrence Gap have some of the most well-known Chattel Villages.

Local Markets: Keep an eye out for local markets, such as Cheapside Market in Bridgetown or Holders Farmers Market, where you can find fresh produce, local crafts, and other unique items.

Bridgetown Shopping: The capital city of Bridgetown offers numerous shopping options, from high-end boutiques to smaller souvenir shops. Broad Street and Swan Street are popular shopping areas.

Tips for Souvenir Shopping:

Bargain: Don't be afraid to haggle a bit, especially at local markets. Vendors might be open to negotiating prices.

Check for Authenticity: When buying local artwork, confirm its authenticity and the artist's name. This adds value to your purchase.

Duty-Free Shopping: Barbados has a strong duty-free shopping scene. Look for duty-free shops at the airport or in Bridgetown to save on luxury items.

Cash and Credit: Many shops accept both cash and credit cards, but it's a good idea to have some local currency on hand for small purchases or at markets.

Shipping Options: If you're concerned about transporting fragile or bulky items, inquire about shipping options to have your purchases sent directly to your home.

Unique Souvenirs:

Local Pottery: Barbadian pottery is known for its intricate designs and bright colors. You can find bowls, plates, and vases adorned with tropical motifs and intricate patterns.

Handmade Soaps and Skincare Products: Look for locally crafted soaps, lotions, and skincare products made from natural ingredients, often inspired by the island's flora and fauna.

Wooden Carvings: Barbadian artisans create beautiful wooden carvings, from small trinkets to larger sculptures. These can be excellent decor items and memorable souvenirs.

Calypso and Reggae Music: Don't forget to bring home some Caribbean beats. Look for CDs or vinyl records of local calypso, reggae, and steelpan music to keep the island's rhythm alive in your home.

Cultural and Historical Items:

Replicas of Historic Sites: Miniature models or artistic representations of Barbados' historic sites, like St. Nicholas Abbey or the Morgan Lewis Windmill, can be great reminders of the island's rich history.

Local Literature: Explore local bookstores for literature written by Barbadian authors or books that delve into the island's history and culture.

Antique Maps: For a unique and historical souvenir, seek out antique maps of Barbados, which can be both decorative and educational.

Best Times to Shop:

Barbados hosts several festivals and events throughout the year that are perfect for souvenir shopping:

Holetown Festival (February): This week-long festival celebrates the arrival of the first English settlers in Barbados and features arts and crafts markets.

Crop Over (July/August): The Crop Over festival, Barbados' biggest cultural event, includes craft markets, music, and colorful costumes. It's an excellent time to explore the local art scene.

Hold a Bargain (Various Dates): Look out for local flea markets and "Hold a Bargain" sales in different neighborhoods. These events often feature a wide range of items at reasonable prices.

Packaging and Shipping:

Packaging: Ensure that delicate items are packaged properly to avoid damage during your journey back home. Many shops will offer to pack items securely.

Shipping Services: If you're concerned about transporting fragile or bulky items, inquire at the point of purchase about shipping options to have your purchases sent directly to your home.

Remember to also take note of Barbados' customs regulations and any duty-free allowances to avoid any unexpected charges upon your departure.

Souvenir shopping in Barbados is not just about acquiring trinkets; it's an opportunity to immerse yourself in the island's vibrant culture, history, and creativity. Whether you're interested in art, food, fashion, or music, Barbados has something to offer, making your shopping experience a memorable part of your visit to this beautiful Caribbean gem.

Chapter 15

Tips and Essential Information for Travelers Visiting Barbados

Barbados, a picturesque island in the Caribbean, is a popular destination for travelers seeking beautiful beaches, vibrant culture, and a rich history. Whether you're planning a relaxing beach vacation or an adventure-filled trip, here are some essential tips and information to make your visit to Barbados enjoyable and memorable.

1. Travel Documents:

Ensure your passport is valid for at least six months beyond your planned departure date.
Visitors from most countries don't require a visa for stays up to 6 months, but check the Barbados Immigration Department's website for specific entry requirements.
2. Best Time to Visit:

Barbados enjoys a tropical climate year-round. The peak tourist season is from December to April, but prices are higher. The off-peak season from May to November offers more budget-friendly options.

3. Accommodation:

Barbados has a wide range of accommodation options, from luxury resorts to boutique hotels and vacation rentals. Book in advance, especially during the peak season.

Popular areas to stay include Bridgetown (the capital), St. Lawrence Gap, and Holetown.

4. Currency:

The official currency is the Barbadian Dollar (BBD), but the U.S. dollar is widely accepted. ATMs are widely available for cash withdrawals.

5. Transportation:

Public transportation is reliable and affordable, with buses and shared taxis (ZRs). Renting a car is an option, but driving is on the left side of the road.

Taxis are readily available, but it's advisable to confirm the fare before starting the journey.

6. Language:

English is the official language of Barbados, so communication won't be a problem.

7. Safety:

Barbados is generally a safe destination. However, like any other place, exercise caution and safeguard your belongings. Avoid walking alone in poorly lit areas at night.

8. Health Precautions:

Ensure your routine vaccinations are up-to-date.
Tap water is safe to drink, but bottled water is widely available.
Use sunscreen and insect repellent, as the sun can be strong, and there might be mosquitos in some areas.

9. Local Cuisine:

Don't miss trying local dishes like "flying fish," "cou cou," and "pepperpot." Explore local markets and street vendors for authentic Barbadian flavors.

10. Activities and Attractions:

Barbados offers a variety of activities such as water sports, snorkeling, diving, hiking, and exploring historic sites like St. Nicholas Abbey and Harrison's Cave.
Visit the beautiful beaches, including Crane Beach, Bathsheba, and Accra Beach.
11. Culture and Festivals:

Barbados is known for its vibrant culture and numerous festivals. Check the calendar for events like Crop Over, Oistins Fish Festival, and Holders Season for music and arts.

12. Shopping:

Shop for local crafts, jewelry, and souvenirs in Bridgetown's duty-free shops and markets.

13. Tipping:

Tipping is not obligatory but appreciated. A 10-15% gratuity is common in restaurants.

14. COVID-19 Considerations:

Keep yourself updated on the latest COVID-19 travel guidelines and entry requirements, which may change over time.

15. Beaches:

Barbados is renowned for its stunning beaches. Crane Beach, with its pink-tinged sands and clear waters, is often considered one of the most beautiful in the world. Other must-visit beaches include Bottom Bay, Accra Beach, and Carlisle Bay.
16. Water Activities:

The island is a paradise for water sports enthusiasts. Try your hand at surfing at Soup Bowl in Bathsheba, go snorkeling or scuba diving to explore vibrant coral reefs, or embark on catamaran cruises for a day of swimming with sea turtles.

17. Wildlife and Nature Reserves:

Animal lovers should visit the Barbados Wildlife Reserve to see green monkeys, iguanas, and various tropical birds in a natural setting. Hike through the

Andromeda Botanic Gardens to witness diverse plant species.

18. Nightlife:

Barbados comes alive at night with a variety of entertainment options. St. Lawrence Gap is known for its lively bars, restaurants, and nightclubs, making it a hotspot for nightlife. You can also enjoy live music and dancing at various venues across the island.

19. Festivals and Events:

Barbados hosts a range of festivals and events throughout the year. Crop Over Festival, the island's largest and most famous event, is a weeks-long celebration with colorful parades, music, and dancing. Check the calendar for other events like the Barbados Reggae Festival and the Barbados Food and Rum Festival.

20. Local Etiquette:

Barbadians are known for their friendliness and politeness. It's customary to greet people with a friendly "good morning" or "good afternoon." When entering homes, remove your shoes as a sign of respect.

21. Environmental Conservation:

Barbados takes its environmental conservation seriously. Join local efforts in keeping the island clean and pristine by disposing of trash properly and respecting marine life and wildlife during your adventures.

22. Day Trips:

Consider taking day trips to nearby islands. For example, a short ferry ride to the Grenadines can provide you with a chance to explore more of the Caribbean's natural beauty.

23. Health Services:

Barbados has a well-developed healthcare system. The Queen Elizabeth Hospital in Bridgetown provides excellent medical care, and there are many private clinics and pharmacies across the island.

24. Emergency Contacts:

In case of emergency, dial 911 for police, medical, or fire assistance.

25. Sustainable Travel:

Support sustainable tourism by choosing eco-friendly accommodations and activities. Respect local culture and nature by minimizing your impact on the environment.

26. Departure and Customs:

Allow sufficient time for check-in and security procedures at the Grantley Adams International Airport. Be aware of customs regulations when departing, especially for duty-free items and souvenirs.

27. Return Visit:

Many travelers find Barbados so enchanting that they return for repeat visits. Consider exploring different areas and experiences during your next trip to the island.

Barbados offers a wealth of experiences for travelers, from its pristine beaches and rich culture to exciting adventures and delectable cuisine. With this comprehensive guide, you're well-prepared to make the most of your trip to Barbados, creating lasting memories of this Caribbean gem. Enjoy your time in paradise!

Chapter 16

14 days itinerary in Barbados, focusing on Sitout and outdoor experience

Day 1: Arrival in Barbados

Arrive at Grantley Adams International Airport in Barbados.
Check into your accommodation on the south coast, known for its beautiful beaches.
Relax by the beach and enjoy a Caribbean sunset.

Day 2: Beach Day

Spend the day at Accra Beach, also known as Rockley Beach.
Enjoy swimming, sunbathing, and water sports.
Explore the boardwalk for a leisurely stroll.

Day 3: Wildlife Adventure

Visit the Barbados Wildlife Reserve in St. Peter.
Observe animals like green monkeys and tortoises in a natural setting.
Have a picnic at Farley Hill National Park.

Day 4: Island Tour

Take a scenic island tour with a local guide.
Visit Harrison's Cave to see stunning underground formations.
Explore the historic sites in Bridgetown.

Day 5: Snorkeling and Catamaran Cruise

Go on a catamaran cruise along the west coast.
Snorkel with sea turtles and explore vibrant coral reefs.
Enjoy a Bajan buffet lunch on board.

Day 6: Hiking in the East Coast

Head to Bathsheba on the rugged east coast.
Hike along the dramatic coastal trails.
Enjoy a picnic at Bathsheba Beach.

Day 7: Watersports

Spend the day at Carlisle Bay.
Try paddleboarding, kayaking, or jet skiing.
Enjoy a beachside barbecue dinner.

Day 8: Relax at Your Accommodation

Take a well-deserved day of relaxation.
Lounge by the pool or on your private sitout.
Enjoy the amenities of your accommodation.

Day 9: Explore Speightstown

Visit the historic town of Speightstown.
Explore Arlington House Museum.
Have lunch at a local seaside restaurant.

Day 10: Nature and Wildlife

Explore Andromeda Botanic Gardens in Bathsheba.
Take a guided hike in Welchman Hall Gully.
Discover unique plant and animal species.

Day 11: Surfing and Beach Day

Take a surfing lesson at the Soup Bowl in
Bathsheba.
Spend the afternoon catching waves or lounging on
the beach.

Day 12: Island Safari

Embark on an island safari tour.
Explore the interior of the island, including lush forests and remote beaches.
Enjoy a traditional Bajan lunch.
Day 13: Zipline Adventure

Experience an adrenaline rush with a zipline adventure in the Scotland District.
Enjoy breathtaking views of the island from above the treetops.
Explore local craft markets.

Day 14: Departure

Spend your last morning at the beach or relaxing at your accommodation.
Reflect on your unforgettable outdoor experiences in Barbados.
Head to the airport for your departure.
This 14-day itinerary provides a perfect balance of outdoor adventures, relaxation, and cultural exploration, allowing you to make the most of your time in beautiful Barbados. Enjoy the natural beauty and warm hospitality of this Caribbean gem!

Printed in Great Britain
by Amazon

31053675R00086